When real-life drama invades the lives of those near us, we marvel at the way adversity can lead to courageous faith. Such is the case in this captivating book that takes you on a wild ride through amusing, heartwarming and tragic family adventures that God used to bring "flannelgraph Jesus" fully alive in a young mom's heart and empowered her to trust His plans when her own plans shattered. The wounds were deep, but the Lord's redeeming grace was deeper still, and His Spirit awakened a buoyant spirit within her that inspires and encourages other. May God's story, woven through this story, inspire you to embrace Him with wide open arms and trust His plan for your life in fearless faith.

—Mary Kay Esswein
MSN, PNP, California State University, Long Beach;
MA Soul Care, Biola University

I have known this writer for many years, and over the last 33 years of our marriage, she is my best friend and buddy. She has been trying to write this story for a long time during her busy life (raising a family, working full time), and finally the Lord said, "Now is the time!" She did not write this story just for people to read another book, but only to praise her Lord and Savior, Jesus Christ. Read it, and you will feel it!

—Bob Keller

Faith, Not Fear is a candid and compelling story on one woman's walk with God through challenging circumstances year after year. Frequently feeling overwhelmed by life, the author places her trust in God's constant love and emerges victorious. It all begins with an unwanted pregnancy—with the author [as a baby about] to be aborted! Thanks to the intervention of a grandmother, the child is rescued by a young Finnish couple and the miracles continue during the years to come. The tender heart of the author brings the reader directly into the presence of the Lord. This is a story for all who have faith in God and yet face difficult times. Enjoy!

—Ray Halm, Ed.D., D.D.
Senior Director, CUEnet;
President Emeritus, Concordia University Irvine

FAITH

[Not Fear]

When it's
God's plan,
you win

CHRISTINE KELLER

Deep River
B O O K S

Published by
Deep River Books
Sisters OR
www.deepriverbooks.com

ISBN: 9781632695284

Library of Congress Control Number: 2020912065

Cover design by Robin Black, Inspirio Design
Printed in the USA

To my savior, Jesus Christ, who has sustained me throughout my journey. His plan for my life has brought me joy, understanding, peace, acceptance, serenity, a strong faith, and the promise of everlasting life in heaven!

To my three daughters, Mary, Sarah, and Anna, who give purpose and meaning to my life. They have shown me God's grace and his unconditional love.

I dedicate this book to you.

CONTENTS

Acknowledgments 9

Introduction 13

   1. An Undivided Heart. 17

   2. An Unlikely Beginning 25

   3. A Sure Foundation 29

   4. A Home-Seeking Heart 39

   5. A Love Redefined 47

   6. A Shifting Wind. 59

   7. A Delicate Sparrow 67

   8. A Song of Hope. 79

   9. A Time to Weep. 89

  10. A Grief Redeemed. 101

  11. A Rose and a Thorn 111

  12. A Word and a Way 119

  13. A Purpose Revealed 127

  14. A Future and a Hope 143

Afterword: Marching Orders. 155

End Notes 163

Precious Photos 164

Acknowledgments

I would like to thank Deep River Books for selecting my manuscript for publication. You gave me a platform to share my story, and your team showed me patience, support, guidance, and enthusiasm. Andy Carmichael, I will be forever grateful for your partnership in this endeavor. I am humbled by your belief in my book!

To my editor, Kit Tosello. God has gifted you with the ability to bring life to my words and create a story. Kit, your skills are incredible and amazing to me. Your crisp finishing touches gave these words wings to fly. I think we make a great team, Kit!

To my daughters, Mary and Anna. Thank you for your technical help. Thank you for believing in *our* story and your old mom.

To Bob, my patient printer. Thank you for your loving support.

"For I know the plans I have for you," declares the
Lord, "plans to prosper you and not to harm you,
plans to give you hope and a future. Then you will
call on me and come and pray to me, and I will listen
to you. You will seek me and find me when you seek
me with all your heart. I will be found by you."

                                    Jeremiah 29:11–14 NIV

There is a time for everything,
and a season for every
activity under the heavens:

a time to be born and a time to die,
a time to plant and a time to uproot,
a time to kill and a time to heal,
a time to tear down and a time to build,
a time to weep and a time to laugh,
a time to mourn and a time to dance,
a time to scatter stones and a time to gather them,
a time to embrace and a time to refrain from embracing,
a time to search and a time to give up,
a time to keep and a time to throw away,
a time to tear and a time to mend,
a time to be silent and a time to speak,
a time to love and a time to hate,
a time for war and a time for peace.

Ecclesiastes 3:1–8 NIV

INTRODUCTION

⁓

In the Bible, the number forty appears significant. It rained for forty days while Noah and his family were in the ark. Jesus was tempted by Satan for forty days. Moses spent forty years in Pharaoh's court, forty years as a fugitive in Midian, and forty years with the Israelites in the desert.

I last attempted to write forty years ago. At that time, I was inspired by my children—and whatever keen insight I possessed at the ripe old age of twenty-six—to pen a poem titled "The Seed of Love." I have always been an old soul, but I like to think I'm a little bit wiser today. For the Lord has decided now is the time for me to write this book.

I'm perplexed that God prompted me to share the story of our journey together. I am no one special, and I certainly have not accomplished anything great. And honestly, I empathize with Job, who ran in the opposite direction of Nineveh to escape God's will. While I'm grateful to report I have never been swallowed by a whale, I have indeed experienced God's wonderful sense of humor. It is comical how he found ways to get my attention when I was running away from his plans.

As I drive to work each morning, I like to tune into Dr. Michael Yousef's "Leading the Way" broadcast. Many times over the years, I heard him express that while God's plans are not always our plans, we need to trust, obey, and lean on Christ. On another Christian station, I often heard Francesca Battistelli sing a song called "Write Your Story." Then, several years ago, my husband, a military veteran, ordered special license plates for his car, the kind with the Army insignia. When they arrived, he said, "Oh dear! I've always memorized my license plate numbers. How am I going to remember this one?"

I looked at the new plates. *GPYW.* "Hmm," I said. "How about *God's Plan, You Win?*"

"Hey, I kinda like that!" he said. "Where did it come from?"

"That, I believe, is the name of the book God wants me to write."

Still, despite the call, I had to work through many excuses not to follow through.

Why would anyone want to read about my life?

This could be embarrassing. People will know how many times I have messed up.

I'm too old and too tired to rehash my life story.

But when God beckons us, his voice is clear, and the mission is urgent. I have heard his voice. I have felt his touch. And I have seen it confirmed that he is aware of every detail of our lives, even the seemingly trivial. God is not some obsolete deity stuck in a dusty, leather-bound book. I know for sure and certain that our Savior is very present to us anytime, anywhere, and in any situation.

I've heard people say the Bible is antiquated and no longer applicable. But God's Word is timeless. His message of love and forgiveness is eternal. And, thanks to the gift of hindsight, I can now see how God's plan for my life fit together like a great, big jigsaw puzzle.

Woe unto those who think God is not real. He is very much alive, and he's preparing to reclaim the sheep who hear his voice. So pay close attention, folks, for as Bob Dylan sang, "the times, they are a-changing." Sometimes God whispers, and sometimes he yells. As I write this, the world is reeling from a global pandemic of unprecedented proportions. We are living in disturbing times—fraught with social upheaval, economic and political tension, wars, and rumors of wars.

As Christians, we're engaged in a spiritual battle unlike any other generation. We need to pray in faith, not fear, knowing God loves us and he's just waiting for us to ask for his help. So we can take a stand for him!

For such a time as this, I believe I've been called to share my journey as a mother to my three daughters. Mine is a tale of overcoming great fear and learning to walk in abiding faith and peace. I'll revisit some mountaintops marked by joyful singing and dancing. And I'll reveal some of my plunges into the dark pits of terror, rage, and desperation. So buckle your seat belt, for here comes the story of Jesus and Chrissy.

May it nourish your faith and reassure you that even in this chaotic world our God is still in control. Jesus sees and hears you, and he walks alongside you. Or perhaps today, he is carrying you. I've been there, my friend.

I pray you will be reminded that with God's plan, you win. And He deserves all the glory.

I will instruct you and teach you in the way you should go; I will counsel you with my loving eye on you.

Psalm 32:8 NIV

1

An Undivided Heart

⟋⟍

For to me to live is Christ, and to die is gain.

Philippians 1:21

My story, the one I came to tell, nearly ended before it began.

But first, let me share someone else's story—a story which, somewhere along the journey, became inseparable from mine.

Faith Like Brianna's

In a few short months we would be moving north to central Oregon, having just sold our family home in Long Beach, California. But first, we had a summer wedding to look forward to, an opportunity to spend joyous hours with many of the treasured friends we'd done life with for nearly forty years.

The invitation hung on the refrigerator in our temporary apartment. The event would be held at our church, Bethany Lutheran, to celebrate the marriage of a young woman in our church, Lindsey. Even better, another dear young friend,

Brianna, would be flying in from Australia to attend Lindsay as a bridesmaid.

For a twenty-five-year-old, Brianna had amassed some impressive credentials and life experience. On top of her bachelors' degree in nursing, she had earned a master's in missions and intercultural studies from Wheaton College in Illinois. She'd attended Focus on the Family Institute in Colorado, an experience she called life-changing, as well as discipleship training school through Youth With a Mission (YWAM) on board the Mercy Ship *Anastasis* in Sierra Leone.

Brianna's many international mission trips had sealed her resolve to serve God on the mission field as a midwife. Having just completed midwife training through YWAM in Perth, Australia, Brianna would fly home for a mere twenty-four-hour visit with family and friends. On the day after the wedding, she would depart for Port Harcourt, Nigeria and join the hospital staff as a midwife missionary nurse.

Being close friends of Brianna's parents, and having known her all her life, I looked forward with eagerness to catching a glimpse of her at the wedding before she embarked on her next far-flung adventure.

⌒

I see Brianna. Her dark hair catches the sunlight as she boards a bus with other missionaries. The atmosphere feels foreign and exotic, but a sweet sense of camaraderie surrounds Brianna and her team. They sing praise songs as they roll along, heading somewhere to serve, full of purpose and joy.

A loud blast splits the air. A fireball erupts—orange and black, angry and roaring—and engulfs the bus. Smoke, a wall of smoke so thick I can no longer see the bus. What's happening?

*"No!" I scream. "Please God, no!" Because, somehow, I'm sure . . .
Brianna is dead.*

*But Bob's here now. He's stroking my arm, talking me down.
I'm in my bed, trying to quiet my nerves and shake off this terrible
sense of foreboding.*

I can't make sense of what I just witnessed.

*But if I'm in my own bedroom, it was all just a dream. Nothing
but a nightmare, a horrific nightmare. Oh, thank God!*

Although I'd never been prone to nightmares, as I considered this dream, I rationalized that its timing made sense. How natural it was for me to harbor concerns about this beautiful young, adventurous woman who was so close to our family and so close in age to my own daughters. Over the years, Brianna's mother, Mary Kay, and I had sung in choir together. We'd been regulars at a weekly gathering for moms, praying our kids and each other through every age and stage. We'd celebrated accomplishments, confided fears and disappointments. We knew each other's hopes and dreams for our children.

Of course, we didn't yet know God's plans for them.

⌒

Lindsey's wedding was truly one of the most beautiful I had ever attended. Bob and I and our daughter Mary drove from the church to the reception at Seal Beach Country Club in Seal Beach, with its exquisite mountain views and rolling green fairways. Lindsey was absolutely breathtaking, a glowing bride! Brianna, her sister, Krista, and the other bridesmaids added to the day's loveliness.

I'm such a hopeless romantic, and I adore weddings. I watched through the clubhouse windows as the sun set, spreading golden light over the golf course where the bride and groom posed for photographs. Later the music began, and I was brought to tears when Lindsey danced with her father, Tom, whose brother is Brianna's father, Dan. Memories flowed—of Lindsey's birth, and of special times I'd shared with her mother, Sheri.

So there I was, enchanted by every detail of the reception on that classically beautiful summer night in southern California—delicious food, glass of white wine, heartwarming toasts, music, flowers. Suddenly, the Lord got my attention, and his voice was unmistakable and urgent.

Get up, Chris. Find Brianna. Tell her about your vision!

Um, are you kidding me?

Get up now. Find Brianna and speak to her about what you saw.

Ahh, that would be a no, Lord. Sorry, but I don't want to. She's only here for a day. She leaves tomorrow. (As if I needed to fill him in on the details.) I refuse to be a Debbie Downer or a Nervous Nellie or a Bring-Me-Down Betty on a day like today. We're celebrating a wedding here. You know, Lord, you attended marriage feasts, and even changed water into wine. And might I remind you that you protested too, when your mother asked it of you? So, no.

Not doing it.

Who was I kidding? God gets what God wants. I felt as if I was literally being lifted away from the comfort of my chair and turned around. Sure enough, there was Brianna with her elegant strapless gown and shining smile. Oh, Lord!

I reached for Brianna and hugged her tight. The Lord was strengthening me. I waited while Brianna and Mary exchanged greetings before taking Bri by the hand and leading her to a more private spot. I was on a mission for God, and I needed to be bold.

The moment felt surreal, as if there was only Bri and me rather than a grand ballroom filled with guests. The music and chatter faded away, leaving us in a sacred space. I took a deep breath, held her hands in mine, and prayed silently for the words.

"Brianna," I began, "I must tell you something. This is a life-and-death message from God. Do not go to Nigeria tomorrow. Please wait for the next assignment."

She looked at me with her stunning blue eyes, appearing puzzled.

I recounted my dream for her, adding that now I understood it had been a vision from God.

"Brianna, you died in the explosion." Now I was crying. "Please don't go on this particular mission trip. There will be other opportunities to serve the Lord!" Even as I pleaded, I could see her firm resistance. She was not going to change her mind.

"Think of your wonderful mother. You two are so close! Please, Bri. I wouldn't have said anything, but the Lord dragged me out of my chair and set you right in front of me."

Brianna reached out and took my face in her hands. Her gaze was intense, and tears shone in her eyes. "I am not afraid to die, Chris. I must go, no matter what awaits me. Jesus has called me to this role, to serve him wherever he needs me. He's called me to Nigeria, and I have to obey."

She wrapped me in a strong hug. "Please don't worry, Chris, just pray for me. You are so precious and caring. I feel your love and concern. But I assure you, I am not afraid!"

Together we cried, then laughed. I kissed her cheek and we parted, saying our goodbyes.

The following morning, Bri flew to Nigeria as planned and stepped confidently into her missionary work. And in the fall,

Bob and I moved to Bend, Oregon as planned, settled into our new digs, and joined a new church. One gloomy Sunday in December, I arrived home after the service feeling a heavy weight. Perhaps it was loneliness, I thought, as I deeply missed the friends we'd left behind. Or maybe I was disappointed because our close friend Doug, the only person we knew when we'd moved to Bend, wasn't at church.

Doug was always such a bright spot in my week during that period of emotional transition, a taste of home. He felt like extended family. He'd been my seventh-grade teacher at Bethany Lutheran and later the school principal. He'd sung in the choir and in a barbershop quartet with my dad and uncle. Sundays in Bend had become our days to reminisce. Yes, that was it. His absence today was probably the source of my mopiness.

I let my purse fall to the kitchen table and considered making Christmas cookies to lift my spirits. But first, a flashing red light on the answering machine caught my eye, signaling a missed phone call. Yay, someone called! I pressed the button.

The sweet voice of my cousin Alicia filled the kitchen, but she sounded upset. "I know you're out of the loop, Chrissy, living so far away," she began. "I . . . I thought you would want to know. Some very sad, devastating news came through our prayer chain this morning. Your dear friend Mary Kay just learned that Brianna has died. She was killed in some kind of a bus accident in Nigeria . . ."

No, no, no! My head buzzed with shock. Dear God, no!

". . . so sorry to have to share this horrible news with you, but I knew you would want to be informed . . ."

I dropped to the kitchen floor. This couldn't be real! Yet somehow, I knew it was.

Oh, poor Mary Kay! I felt the stake being driven through her heart as if it was my own. I heard a guttural scream, then realized it was coming from me.

Bob came running, eyes wide. "Honey . . . What? What is it?" He reached to help me up, but I was anchored to the floor. "Tell me, Chrissy. What's happened?"

I reminded him of my vision. "Oh, my God. Bob, it's happened. Brianna died in a bus accident. This morning!"

I'd failed in my assignment to protect her. Now Mary Kay's heart was forever broken. Why, Lord? What gives? Why give me a prophetic vision about Bri, but not the power to make her change her plans? I'm angry! Talk to me!

This wasn't about you, Child. Brianna loved me with a pure faith. Her life and her death, both were destined to bring me glory.

But Lord, she had her whole life ahead of her, and she wanted to serve you with it.

Your work is to tell her story, so others may live out their faith as she did.

Over time, I learned to see divine purpose in the way Bri's faith walk intersected with mine. Our sweet, beautiful, Jesus-adoring young woman was gone. Yet her face at the wedding reception would be ever before me. Her fearless gaze as she insisted she had no intention of abandoning her calling. Her God-confidence, so solid and contagious that I had no choice but yield in the face of such conviction.

They say fear is the absence of faith, that the two can't coexist in the same moment, within the same heart. Over the years since that fateful December, Brianna's unwavering trust in God's plan—whether it meant a long earthly life, or short—remains for me a picture of the kind of faith Jesus asked of his disciples. The kind I aspire to.

Her story adds perspective to mine. I see clearly now how, in every chapter, God has been teaching me to walk the way his darling child Brianna did—in faith, not fear.

And that it comes at a cost.

2

AN UNLIKELY BEGINNING

"Whoever humbles himself like this child is the greatest in the kingdom of heaven. Whoever receives one such child in my name receives me."

Matthew 18:4–5

On a hot and sticky summer night in Wisconsin in 1951, a couple of college students unintentionally conceived a baby. They'd been dating for two years or so, and when the pregnancy was confirmed, the father said, "Let's get married."

The girl's domineering mother, however, was having none of that. Her daughter was not to marry the boy, and the baby was not to be born. "Tell him it was a false alarm, and break things off with him," she decreed. "We will not discuss this any further." An appointment was made for the abortion.

My fate was sealed, it seemed. I was simply a product to be disposed of.

And yet, had an ultrasound been done, they might have seen that I was a well-formed, flesh-and-blood girl, roughly the size of a large avocado and complete with every important organ including a heart that had already been beating for several months. I had vocal cords and teeth, and I could move my eyes. I already had my very own, one-of-a-kind fingerprints and well-formed ears. I could even hear their voices, making life-or-death plans. And here's where the plot twists.

> *For you formed my inward parts; you knitted me together in my mother's womb.*
>
> Psalm 139:13

What these Wisconsin folks didn't know was that for sixteen weeks, while they had been deciding my fate, God was penning the first glorious words of my story. And the first chapter was to feature a rescue.

In swooped the young pregnant woman's grandmother, guiding her to a different solution. There would be no abortion. Instead, she would whisk her granddaughter away to sunny Long Beach, California, where they would rent an apartment for the duration of the pregnancy. They'd choose an obstetrician and hire an attorney to arrange for the baby's adoption.

Once they returned to Wisconsin, there would be no further mention of the incident—and certainly no tears. Since the grandmother had means, the parties involved could easily explain away the long absence by saying they'd undertaken an extended European cruise.

⁓

Nine years earlier, on Valentine's Day of 1942, Mickey and Hilda Lundi began their married life. Mickey, an engineer who hailed from Ohio, had served in the merchant marines on the Great Lakes during World War II. Hilda was a registered nurse, raised on her parents' working farm in Maple, Wisconsin.

Both Mickey and Hilda were full-blooded Finnish, and proud of it. They spoke the language and could read and write in Finnish as well.

After marrying, they moved first to New York City, following work opportunities. But soon, tired of the freezing weather, they packed up and migrated to Long Beach, California to enjoy the warmth and sunshine. Both had siblings who had already settled into communities close to one another in southern California.

But once in California, hard times fell their way. All of their earthly belongings, including family heirlooms and wedding gifts, were stolen by the moving company. Despite filing a claim, they never got back their precious things.

Hilda got pregnant but miscarried. In the process, doctors discovered she had uterine cancer. At the young age of twenty-four, Hilda underwent a complete hysterectomy followed by radiation. On the up side, the radiation worked, and the cancer never returned.

Dr. Hartley, one of the obstetricians who practiced at Seaside Hospital in Long Beach (now Long Beach Memorial Hospital), where Hilda worked in the neonatal intensive care nursery, knew Hilda's story. A baby lost. A cancer fight won. The death of her dream of bearing children.

Dr. Hartley knew another woman's story as well. A young female patient from Wisconsin who was preparing to surrender her child for adoption.

And so it happened, smooth as a baby's bottom. Mickey and Hilda arranged for a closed adoption, meaning the court records would be sealed tight, so that the birth mother would have no information about or contact with the child or her parents.

Nevertheless, Hilda, unbeknownst to the birth mom, found a clever way to be in the delivery room when I was born. Little did the young woman from Wisconsin know that the nurse who handed her the consent form to sign, legally transferring her parental rights to Mickey and Hilda, was Hilda herself.

How like my mom to arrange things her own way! Over the years to come, she often enjoyed recalling how she "pulled a fast one" in the delivery room on the day I arrived.

And so I went straight from the body of my biological parent into my mother's arms in early March of 1952.

I can only scratch my head when I consider the remarkable "coincidence" of my adoptive parents finding their way from Wisconsin to a small hospital in Long Beach, California, where their lives intersected with mine, having made the same journey under very different circumstances.

How can I not feel anything but amazed and blessed? From Day One, God had been perfectly knitting me together and arranging every circumstance—whether hard or happy—for my good and his glory.

> *But when Jesus saw it, he was indignant and said to them, "Let the children come to me; do not hinder them, for to such belongs the kingdom of God."*
>
> Mark 10:14

3

A Sure Foundation

~~~

It is better to take refuge in the LORD than to trust in man.

<div align="right">Psalm 118:8</div>

" Chrissy Emi," my dad liked to tease, "the day you blew into Long Beach sure was memorable!" Evidently a howling windstorm picked up on the day I was born, featuring some of the wildest gusts he had ever experienced. Then, out of the chaos, a happy and harmonious tempo settled over the Lundi home. After ten years of marriage, Mickey and Hilda were parents.

Family Footings

My mom and dad were good, steady, middle-class Americans. They stood for God, country, and family. They believed in education and hard work. In fact, they were so upstanding that the county adoption social worker encouraged them to add to their family. Nearly three years after I arrived, they adopted a boy—my brother, Juss, which is Finnish for John. And a few years later, they added another girl—my sister, Elisabeth, who we call Liz. Now we were a family of five.

Although denied the houseful of full-blooded Finnish children they had hoped for, my parents made a comfortable, lively, musical home for us. In 1954, we settled into a modest, new ranch house, where we remained for all our growing-up years. Later we added on a beautiful family room.

Every morning, as I followed the scent of oatmeal or cinnamon rolls down the hallway, I'd pass a cluster of family photos, along with Fleur Conkling's poem known to many as the *Adoption Creed*.

> *Not flesh of my flesh*
> *nor bone of my bone,*
> *but still miraculously my own.*
> *Never forget for a single minute,*
> *you didn't grow under my heart,*
> *but in it!*

As chance would have it, my dad was a homebody, but his work required he be gone a lot, while my stay-at-home mom longed to travel. During the week, when dad was gone on his construction jobs, Mom kept house, led John's Cub Scout pack as well as our Girl Scout troops, and sewed our Halloween costumes. She was a gifted seamstress.

Oh, how we all looked forward to the weekends! On Fridays, once the house was in order, Mom set her hair in curlers for "date night." With his work week done, fun seemed to follow Dad through the kitchen door. Always he came bearing treats, typically Good & Plenty candies or a bag of M&Ms.

After handing things off to the babysitter, my parents departed for their favorite restaurant. And following dinner, they moved to the lounge, where Dad sang at the piano bar with his gorgeous bass voice.

Meanwhile at home, my siblings and I were scooched around our big, circular coffee table, the one you could spin like a great big lazy Susan, while *The Flintstones* and *Rawhide* played on the television. We liked to pour out all our candies on the table, separate them by color, and then spin the table, grabbing just one candy at a time.

That beloved table stayed in the family. Today it lives with my niece Amy in her New York City home.

We always knew when the milkman was in the neighborhood, his arrival heralded by the loud rattle of all those glass bottles. Sometimes we were allowed chocolate milk as a special treat. On Saturdays, the Helm Bakery truck came around. We'd all run outside and excitedly choose our one donut.

Throughout summer, Mom and Dad hosted barbecues, often with a theme, such as "luau." Dad would be in his sweet spot, supervising a large prime rib on the spit, while all the teachers and pastors from our school and church gathered with their families for food, games, and singing. Always, there was music. And when *The Lawrence Welk Show* came on, we closed out our Saturday nights watching our parents dance the polka.

In our home, dancing, like singing, was considered timeless. And biblical, even. So my parents enrolled me in ballet very young. By eight years old, I'd fallen in love with the Nutcracker ballet and was dancing *en pointe*.

As musical families go, we rivaled the von Trapps. There were a lot of us—aunts, uncles, and cousins on both sides. Dad regular sang harmony with his siblings, and barbershop quartet. For over fifty years, he regularly dueted with my mom's brother, Uncle Evert, in the Bethany Lutheran church choir. Dad's dedication to choir set a wonderful example for us children. If he could drive home from his construction job, he would do so every Thursday evening, so as not to miss choir practice. Early Friday morning, he'd have to travel the distance back to the job site and then circle back home again that evening.

Occasionally Dad allowed the living room to be the venue for our "neighborhood band." I would play the piano, my brother, the trombone, and my sister, the comb—even though it made her lips tingle. Joining us was one of my lifelong best friends, Gloria, usually on spoons, along with her brothers Larry and Alan, and sometimes our across-the-street neighbors, Jay and Shanna.

For drums, Larry would lug in a couple of trash cans and turn them upside-down on the living room carpet! My parents would even join in—Dad on his ukulele, Mom on the triangle. With a little imagination, we never wanted for "instruments." Dad and his brothers had even created a homemade bass fiddle by stringing a thick rope through a washbasin.

Gloria, or "Gleor" as I've always called her, lived right behind us at the time. Alan is an excellent clarinet player to this day.

Mom and Dad had open hearts and an open front door. For a time, two of Dad's brothers, Uncle Butch and Uncle Marvin, lived with us. So did Jeff, a close family friend who was a music major at Cal State Long Beach.

Jeff was part Finnish, and he too hailed from a musical family. His parents often sang with my dad and the "family singers." A dedicated trombone player, Jeff practiced all the time—enough so that our neighbors complained. So Jeff had to hike down to where Interstate 405 was under construction and practice his horn below the overpass. If someone rang the home phone offering Jeff a trombone gig, it was my job to jump on my bike and ride like lightning down to the underpass. While Jeff pedaled quickly home to take the call, I'd balance on the handlebars with his trombone. We may have looked pretty funny, but Jeff's dedication paid off. He grew up and played trombone with the Los Angeles Philharmonic.

In a way, music cemented us all together. But even more importantly, my parents were laying for me a foundation that was eternal and sure. They were building our home on the Rock.

Stormproof

"Everyone then who hears these words of mine and does them will be like a wise man who built his house on the rock. And the rain fell, and the floods came, and the winds blew and beat on that house, but it did not fall, because it had been founded on the rock."

Matthew 7:24–25

Little did I know as a young girl rehearsing these words of Jesus how true they would prove out in years to come. Although I wouldn't encounter the Lord on a deeply personal level until I was well into adulthood, the seed of faith had been planted. A seed that might easily have been whisked away at the first sign of storm without the solid faith community and teaching that marked my early years.

But I couldn't yet know how, when the rains began falling, he would comfort me. Or that one day, in a fearsome deluge of anguish, I'd feel him close by my side. I hadn't experienced how he would tenderly lift my chin and speak to me in the storms.

For now, our church and faith community were central to family life. My dad's sister Ethel and her husband, my Uncle Larry, a Lutheran minister, became my godparents. I was baptized and confirmed at Bethany Lutheran and attended parochial school through eighth grade. And I made many friends there—some of them, lifelong girlfriends, like Juddie and Robin.

Between Gloria, Juddie, and Robin, I've been blessed beyond measure. By and by, whenever storm clouds gathered, these friends remained. To lean on. And to laugh with.

Dad and Mom were energetically involved in our church and school. Mom wrote plays for Sunday school and directed the Nativity pageant every December, even sewing the costumes. A very capable administrator, she took charge of Vacation Bible School, always first to arrive and last to leave. How my siblings and I griped about it at the time.

Later, the man from Galilee in whose name we prayed would jump off that Sunday-school felt board and weave his way deep into my heart. Much later, reflecting on my life as an overcomer, my heart would overflow with gratitude for the healthy church culture my parents cultivated, which framed my growing-up years. Clearly, aside from providing me with a home and family, my parents gave me *the* greatest, most enduring gift.

But back then, it was simply our way of life.

Wearing the Wrong Genes

Still, no parents are perfect, and, alas, mine were no exception. While Dad and I remained close over the years, my relationship with my mother grew strained.

Perhaps if I'd been Finnish, we all could have avoided a great deal of heartache.

Sometimes the words slipped out from Mom, God bless her. Words that beat me down. Unlike my dad, who was my soft place to land and who made me feel like I could be the next American president if I put my mind to it, mom was often domineering and sharp-tongued. Over time, I would learn to recognize that her misdirected bitterness, as well as her growing dependency on alcohol, arose from insecurities and hurts I knew nothing about.

Nevertheless, as an impressionable young girl, here's what I heard:

> *If we could've had our own children, they would be much smarter than you.*
>
> *You got a B?! Tsk, tsk. I never got a B.*
>
> *Notice how all your Finnish cousins were valedictorians?*

My soft, empathetic nature at times even irked my dad. This was not the Finnish way! And there was the rub.

I wasn't *sisu* enough.

Historically, the Finnish people have prided themselves on embodying a certain kind of formidability, an attitude of persistence and determination developed during the early years of their country's formation. Finns are nothing if not sisu (pronounced see-soo)—strong of will, stoic, rational in the face of adversity.[1]

Case in point: my paternal grandmother. In 1914, at the age of eighteen, Grandmother Anna decided to follow her sister and brother-in-law who had immigrated to America in search of a better life, as had many Finnish families in the early twentieth century. Anna Sofia Turja agreed to the journey, enticed by a job with her brother-in-law. He booked her passage.

On the maiden voyage of the *RMS Titanic*.

Indeed, the remarkable fact that Grandmother Anna was among the few third-class passengers who survived the doomed voyage must be credited to her strong Finnish sisu. And by extension, so does my father's very existence. (I marvel when people ask me, "Did your grandmother survive?")

Late on the night of April 14, as Anna was settling into her berth in the belly of the ship, she felt a great shudder and shake. Moments later, her roommate's brother hammered on their door, shouting a warning of eminent disaster. Unlike others who fainted, Grandmother was unafraid.[2] By all accounts, she remained calm and steady, dressing in warm clothes and climbing the stairs to the upper decks.

When a crew member ordered her to stay below deck, she and her Finnish roommates refused to obey. The crew member relented. But he abruptly closed and chained the doors behind them, preventing other third-class passengers from following.

As the band famously played on, Anna listened, enchanted. Between the music and the language barrier, which prevented her from understanding what all the activity really meant, she was able to reassure herself that the ship was unsinkable, and descended to what turned out to be the boat deck, where the air wasn't so cold. There, a sailor picked her up and carried her to one of the last two lifeboats.[3]

Anna's hard-nosed determination, it would seem, had allowed her to be in the right place at the right moment, rather than among the fifteen-hundred-plus passengers who perished in the frigid North Atlantic Ocean on that fateful night. But she would always be haunted by their cries.

After arriving to a great deal of fanfare, Grandma started a new life in Ashtabula, Ohio, home to a large Finnish community. She fell in love with her brother-in-law's brother, Emil Lundi, and the couple raised seven children. My father was their oldest. A quiet, petite woman who adored roses, Grandma Anna lived to eighty-seven and is remembered as someone who exuded God's love and gentleness. And, apparently, sisu.

To my parents' chagrin, however, the Finnish attitude so integral to my family heritage simply wasn't in my genes. But where my family perceived a deficiency, my Creator did not. God had formed my tender heart for his sovereign purposes. He'd fashioned me with everything I'd need to fulfill my destiny—and His power, to boot. I was already more than enough.

No, my parents weren't perfect. Who is this side of heaven? But I'll always be thankful they set me on a solid foundation and pointed me to a perfect savior.

4

A HOME-SEEKING HEART

Delight yourself in the LORD, and he will give you the desires of your heart.

Psalm 37:4

The trouble with a tender heart is learning to protect its edges.

Mine was open wide and in search of a place to land. A place to love boldly and be loved. A place of purpose. But I was a Grade-A marshmallow, headed for a painful learning curve.

I met Tom when I was a high school sophomore and he was a senior. One fall day in 1967, I came upon my friend Kathy chatting with a very tall, very good-looking guy. I crossed campus, wearing my favorite green sleeveless above my stirrup pants and crisp white tennies, to get a closer look. In those days, I wore my brown hair short for swim team.

Kathy introduced us, explaining that she knew Tom from the ranch where they both boarded their horses. Pitch-black hair. Striking green eyes. An amateur bull rider in rodeo. I didn't know much about horses or rodeo, but I liked this six-foot-two cowboy instantly.

Although Tom and I clicked, I wasn't yet allowed to date. When I asked if I could accept his invitation to a football game, my parents told me, "Absolutely not. But you may take the rooter bus and sit with your friends." One Friday night after a game, he invited me to pizza. Since we'd be joining up with other friends there, my folks deigned to let me go but dictated a strict 10:30 p.m. curfew.

Unlikely as it sounds, Tom got lost trying to find the Shakey's Pizza parlor, and we ended up just driving around. Not only did we not get to eat pizza, but we missed my curfew by a mile. When he walked me to the door, I knew there would be an ugly scene with my folks. There was.

Nevertheless, Tom wanted to see me again. So my parents came up with what they thought was an appropriate arrangement. Tom could come over once a week. We could sit in the living room with the whole family. And we were to occupy opposite ends of the couch. Surprisingly, he tolerated this and made the best of it. He and my dad both loved fishing, and they enjoyed chatting about that. Mom was less enthusiastic. She had someone else in mind for me, someone with higher college and career aspirations.

Still, I was gah-gah. And when Tom came by one day, green eyes sparkling, and presented me with a generous gift, I was a goner. Walking on air and hugging the two shiny-new record albums—Smokey Robinson, and The Turtles—I entered the kitchen.

"You have to give those back," Mom said, looking up from her paper.

"What? Why?"

"There's only one thing an older boy like him wants. If you won't give them back, I will."

I was incensed. Never had I talked back to my folks. But never had Tom even tried to kiss me. She was wrong. "No!" I screamed.

Still, the next time Tom came over to watch TV, I handed the albums to him. "I'm sorry," I said. "Mom says you're older than me, and you only want one thing."

Later when I passed Mom again in the kitchen, venom rose to my lips. "I hate you," I said, storming off. And I did, for a while.

After Tom graduated, he gave junior college a try. Meanwhile, perhaps as an outlet for his anger over his father's death and his mother's recent remarriage, he kept entering dangerous rodeo events. Although his new stepfather, Paul, was a kind man, Tom wanted nothing to do with this new family dynamic.

I, on the other hand, did. Badly. For me, his mom, Helen, was the soft place to land I didn't know I'd been seeking. I gravitated to this kind, steady mother figure. A teetotaling Nazarene from the Bible belt and survivor of childhood polio, Helen walked with the help of leg braces. But those braces hadn't destroyed her spirit. She was beautiful and tenacious and somehow carried herself with remarkable grace. And she adored me.

Paul was sweet to the bone and good to her. When Helen needed new clothes, Paul would happily venture out to Bullock's department store, or Buffum's. He'd purchase an array of lovely garments for her to try on at home, and traipse back to the stores to return those she rejected.

Tom's frustration continued. In a match of wills against a twenty-three-hundred-pound Brahma bull named Wimpy, Tom was hurled to the ground and sustained broken bones and internal injuries. Eventually, his disillusionment drove him away from home, and he enlisted for four years in the Air Force. Before he left for boot camp, I presented him with a cross necklace and promised to write.

I kept that promise, penning letters to Tom, who was seeing action in Vietnam, even as I graduated high school and accepted invitations to date other young men. I also clung to my friendship with Helen.

In 1972, Tom flew home on leave, along with his dog named Honey Girl. He phoned me in the middle of the night and asked me to pick him up from LAX, so he could surprise his mom for her birthday. Helen asked me to spend the day with them.

Although Tom was still stationed in Myrtle Beach, South Carolina, he was due to be discharged in December. Before Vietnam, Tom had been an intense young man with a body physically ravaged by rodeo. Now, at twenty-five, he was a total train wreck. Anxious, angry, broken in every way. Not that I was a perfect angel, but Tom was clearly messed up, the way he was drinking and drugging.

At the time, I was attending Cal State University at Long Beach and had just been through a painful breakup. Tom asked if I was seeing anyone, and I said no. But Tom's choices made me uncomfortable. My friends and I had managed to navigate the sixties and seventies without falling into the drug scene, and after being around my mom's drinking, I'd had enough of that lifestyle.

One day while I was at work, nannying for a little boy, Helen called me. "Oh, Chris, can you help Tommy? He needs you," she pleaded.

I found him sitting in his living room with a bottle of whiskey. I told him, "I will not be a part of this destructive lifestyle you're leading."

He reached out and clung to me. "Don't leave me. If I get off the drugs and alcohol, will you date me when I get out of the service?" A compelling offer to a softhearted rescuer like me.

My heart responded as if to a homing beacon. I told Tom I'd wait for him.

And true to his word, he came home clean and stayed clean. In February, we talked about marriage. Technically, he never actually asked for my hand; we just sort of agreed to it. He did, however, ask my father for his blessing. Dad granted it. But when Mom heard, she was furious and flew out of the house, slamming the front door behind her.

Tom and I were married the following May.

Even though he wasn't Mom's choice for a son-in-law, Tom was a good man who had served his country, and he was willing to work hard. Besides, I got Helen in the bargain! And she got me. Tom had a brother named Jerry—yes, like the cartoon characters—but I was the daughter Helen never had.

As sad as it sounds, I would later reflect that I married Tom because I so dearly loved his mother. And I stayed with him longer than was healthy for either of us because I didn't want to hurt her.

In Helen, my heart had found a place of belonging. And in Tom, I'd been given the hope of family. In casting a vision for the future, he and I shared the same dream. We would raise children, and I would be a stay-at-home mom. We had a plan!

By December of '74, Tom and I had settled into a new house in Rowland Heights, a thirty-minute jaunt up the freeway from Long Beach. Thanks to Tom's care, our lawn was something of a neighborhood wonder. Often I'd answer the doorbell to find some random passerby standing there. "Say, what kind of seed is your lawn planted with?" they would ask.

I had no clue. I just knew it was soft and pretty and I could easily imagine playing on it someday with our baby. If possible, when it came to the dream of babies, Helen's excitement practically rivaled mine. Meanwhile, I worked at the same water softener factory where Helen now kept the books, and continued with classes at CSULB.

The plan—my plan, anyway—seemed right on track. I'd graduate, then go full throttle into motherhood.

A Happy Surprise

I hadn't exactly planned to be lactating on the day of my college graduation, new-mama's milk bleeding through the front of my gown as I crossed the podium. But that's how it went down.

The previous fall, just as classes were starting, I'd dipped into the CSULB health center to confirm my suspicions. I was greeted by, of all people, my dear childhood friend Robin, who worked there. She ran the pregnancy test I requested and then had to keep her findings secret from me until the doctor could deliver the news. Even while she sat waiting with me, joining me in giggles of anticipation, she never let on.

Indeed, I was expecting.

But I also had a load of classes to complete in order to graduate. This was a problem. I'd promised Mom and Dad that I wouldn't let anything get in the way of my bachelor's degree. Still anxious to please them, I obtained special permission to carry twenty-four units in order to finish by the end of December. If I poured on the afterburners, I'd be able to walk with my class the following spring. A promise was a promise, after all. And I was motivated.

Helen's needle started flying. Talented in embroidery and fabric arts, she began quilting and cross-stitching baby items like there was no tomorrow. One piece of wall art she created for the nursery read,

> *Cleaning and scrubbing can wait till tomorrow.*
> *For babies grow up, we've learned to our sorrow.*
> *So quiet down cobwebs. Dust go to sleep.*
> *I'm rocking my baby, and babies don't keep.*

I was a woman obsessed, seeking wisdom . . . with a side of humor. I titled my final, sixty-minute project for speech class "Motherhood: The Good, the Bad, and the Beautiful." In it, I quoted comedian Erma Bombeck, the Bible, and a host of other sources. I sensed I was on the brink of my dream come true.

How was I to know how *very* good, *very* beautiful, and yet excruciatingly hard a dream could be?

5

A LOVE REDEFINED

~~~

We love because he first loved us.

1 John 4:19

"Oh my goodness, the baby just kicked!" Startled, I set down my soup spoon.

Helen and I had just returned from Christmas shopping, where I'd purchased the first nativity scene for our home and Helen had picked out some more grandma-goodies—craft projects to work on for the baby. We were in her living room enjoying a bowl of Helen's mm-mm-good homemade vegetable soup.

"Of course it did," Paul teased. "They do that, you know."

Helen shot him a look that implied, *Party pooper!*

The baby kicked again, and Helen's delicious warm soup splashed around in my growing tummy. I squealed with delight.

Helen let out one of her wonderful belly laughs. I guided her hand to the place I'd felt movement, and tears of joy shone in her eyes. She felt it too.

I couldn't wait to tell Tom when he got off work.

Having always loved Christmas, I was enchanted to find that this year it was even more magical. The music chimed sweeter and lights sparkled brighter. Our planned family gatherings and feasts and candlelight services to celebrate our Savior's birth held an extra dose of anticipation. My siblings and Tom's were still in their teens, so this child growing in my womb would be the first grandchild on both sides of the family. None of my closest girlfriends, Juddie, Gloria, and Robin, had children yet.

Tom and I ventured out to the foothills and cut down our own tree. Due to my serious phobia of spiders and, well, all things that creep and crawl, this new tradition was a stretch for me. I was terrified some creature that was supposed to live outdoors might make its way into our home. So Tom patiently hosed down the tree and let it set out to dry before bringing it across the threshold.

On Christmas morning, an elegant dark-oak rocking chair magically appeared in our living room. A gift from Tom, the chair had been wrapped by Helen in a huge red bow and secreted into our house by soon-to-be-grandpa Paul. From my parents, we received a beautiful cradle.

Would our child be a boy or girl? We had no preference and liked the element of surprise. *Just healthy, please.* To keep things neutral, we decided to decorate the baby's room in beige, with ecru curtains and a crib of dark wood. We trimmed the wallpaper with a playful Raggedy Ann and Andy border.

Three baby showers later, I was aglow with all the attention from extended family. My cousin Alicia hand-painted a familiar prayer on a plaque for the nursery. "Now I lay me down to sleep. I pray the Lord my soul to keep. Guard me, Jesus, through the night, and wake me with the morning light." The words seemed to bathe the room in safety. Rhythmic, rhyming, and easy to remember.

A day was coming when my prayers would lean more to the ragged and raw, if I was able to pray at all.

Yet, had I eyes into the future, I'd have been amazed that nearly fifty years later, as I wrote this book, that plaque would adorn my grandson's room. At the time it was more than enough to know my long-dreamed-of baby would soon occupy our home.

With motherhood as my highest aspiration, I'd never desired to be a career woman. Nevertheless, I hung in at my job until a week before my due date. I could climb any mountain, knowing I'd soon hold my child.

On Saturday, May 3, 1975, Tom hobbled off the field after a recreational softball game, nursing a severe knee injury. Still, that evening, we accepted an invitation from our across-the-street neighbors, Jan and Gary, for a barbeque. Jan was a career gal and, other than me, the only woman on our block who worked outside the home.

Jan and Gary were also different from the other young couples around us in that they had no kids. Everyone else seemed to be starting families. I took every opportunity to get to know the neighbors, to observe how they fixed up their homes and yards and how they parented.

I felt well when I left the barbecue, although I hadn't been hungry. Around 2:00 in the morning, I awoke thinking I must have wet my bed. On closer inspection, my water had broken. Oh, joy, today we would be having a baby!

Tom quickly had phone in hand and was relaying my obstetrician's questions. "Having any contractions?" he asked.

"Not yet," I said.

Dr. Meals suggested we try to get some more rest and plan to drive to the hospital in the morning. Despite the excitement and his worsening knee pain, Tom managed to get back to sleep. I was much too worked up.

I showered, washed my long head of hair, and even shaved my legs. You would have thought I was getting ready to go to the prom. Well, I was getting ready to meet my child! Opening the little suitcase I had packed for the hospital, I deliberated about which outfit to dress the baby in for his or her homecoming.

By 8:00 a.m., I'd curled my hair, applied mascara and lip gloss, and was looking across the kitchen table at Tom, thinking, *I don't feel so great anymore.* I'd been having contractions and they were not comfortable. "We'd better get to the hospital," I finally said, knowing we still had to drive to Long Beach.

When we arrived at Long Beach Community Hospital, the head nurse said, "Where have you guys been? We've been waiting!" I didn't realize they'd been expecting us to arrive much earlier.

By now, Tom couldn't stand for long without his knee swelling up and killing him. Until 4:40 p.m. he focused on writing down all my contractions on a scrap of paper, one that I'd keep forever. About the time my contractions became hard to handle, in walked my mom like she owned the place. This was indeed her turf. For many years, she had worked as a registered nurse and an administrator at this very hospital. I opened my eyes to find her with two adorable Disney figurines. One was Minnie Mouse in a pink dress, and the other was Mickey Mouse in all blue. Mom knew I loved Disneyland. After depositing a quick kiss on my cheek, she was gone.

Now the hard work began. My contractions were right on top of each other. Despite Lamaze breathing, the pain became so great I was hyperventilating. When I could no longer feel my hands or feet, someone slapped an oxygen mask on me. Suddenly a powerful urge to push overcame me.

Back in those days, at this stage, the hospitals would transfer the woman from a labor room into the delivery room to give birth. There you were, fully dilated and in the throes of trying not to push, being asked to heft your great big body onto an ice-cold metal cart. They strapped you in and set your hands on two frigid handles. Finally, they'd say, "Okay. Now, with the next contraction, you may push."

Alrighty then, let's do this, Lord. Tom lifted me up, and with two great pushes, Mary Christine made her debut at 6:41 p.m. We'd done it, and without an epidural or any pain medicine. At seven pounds, four ounces and twenty-one inches long, Mary was perfect!

Tom soon disappeared, returning a short while later from the hospital gift shop beaming with pride and joy and carrying several sweet, feminine dresses. We had a girl!

Grandma Helen and Grandpa Paul arrived after Sunday-evening church service. I looked lovingly at Helen, radiant in her sapphire-blue knit long-sleeve dress with a silver brooch on the shoulder and reached for her hand. "Wait till you see Mary. She is sooo pretty!"

Helen could hardly contain her excitement at having a granddaughter. "I've always wanted to have a reason to go to Luan's Little Girls' Dress Shop!" she confided. Over the next few years, Helen would become one of their regular customers.

"For it is Mary, Mary . . . a grand old name," Daddy sang out, when he was introduced to his first grandchild. This became his theme song for her.

Tom and I phoned my dear cousin Jill and her hubby, Glenn, to ask if they would be godparents for Mary. They joyfully agreed. A sacred circle was complete: Jill's parents, my Uncle Larry (a reverend) and Aunt Ethel are my godparents. And Tom and I are godparents to Jill and Glenn's firstborn son, Jeff.

By day three, we expected to take Mary home. But parenthood threw us our first curve ball. Admittedly, I was a hormonal and overly emotional new mother. So when we learned we would have to leave Mary behind because she was jaundiced, I was devastated. After being discharged, I stayed with my parents, who lived close to the hospital, and drove there to nurse her every three hours around the clock.

There would be no shortage of breast milk for Mary. My obstetrician even compared me to a Jerseymaid cow. To me, my milk was practically holy milk, and I pumped like there was no tomorrow. Under no circumstances was a drop to be thrown out. Once I filled a bowl with it and gave it to my beloved cat Buttons as a treat. After lapping at it just once, all the fur stood up on his back. He meowed loudly and ran off. I didn't know whether to laugh or cry at such rejection.

At least poor Tom was more sensitive to my feelings. When I insisted he try my breast milk on his cereal, he pronounced it warm and sweet. Perhaps I had found an outlet for all this milk! I was even able to donate some to the hospital nursery.

Then came the next curve ball. Tom's orthopedic surgeon insisted he needed surgery on his knee right away. While Mary was still under the lights at Long Beach Community Hospital for jaundice, Tom was admitted there as a surgery patient.

Breastfeeding gave me a voracious appetite. Too bad no one had bothered to tell me that I should limit my chocolate intake for the baby's sake. So while I sat in the hospital keeping Tom company, I'd munch on the candy bars so conveniently available

from the vending machine. Poor little Mary became miserable.
I'd made her constipated.

Here was a new feeling. So this was what it felt like to be
the world's most awful mom. Lesson learned. *Lord, forgive me.
Teach me.*

Some lessons ahead would not be as easily dismissed.

At last, our little family of three made it out of the hospital
together. In those days before strict infant car seat laws were
enforced, I was able to hold my tightly swaddled baby in my
arms. Looking over at Tom behind the wheel, taking us home to
begin our family's future, I felt a deep sense of gratefulness and
peace. I was blessed.

The Nirvana-like feelings were short-lived, however. Even
as I learned to meet the around-the-clock needs of a brand-new
infant, I was also in constant demand by a bedridden Tom.
Whenever he took a shower, I would have to wrap his long leg
from head to groin with Saran Wrap to keep his cast dry. Then
I'd breastfeed Mary, buckle her in her little seat, and run into
the kitchen to check on whatever I had on the stove. But wait—
there was Tom's voice again, yelling for help with getting out of
the shower, unwrapping his leg, and drying it off.

One day Tom commented on how nice things had been
in the hospital, how wonderful it had felt to climb from the
shower each day into clean sheets. Would I, he asked, put fresh
sheets on our king-sized bed whenever he was in the shower?
Okay, I thought. *The poor man is recovering from surgery. He's in
pain. He's on temporary disability. I can do this!*

Each day, I did my best to keep up. Feed Mary. Change
her diapers. Tote meals and medications to the surgery patient.
Wash and dry the sheets. Change the bed again. Maybe I *did*
have the stuff of Wonder Woman.

I suppose everyone has their breaking point. First, self-pity seeps in, washing gratitude to the curb. *What happened to the joy and honor of new motherhood? I've just given birth. Aren't I allowed to put my feet up now and then?* Then one day, the proverbial straw breaks the camel's back.

Eventually, the day came when Tom took things too far. "Chrissy, would you please sterilize my toothbrush?" he said.

I kid you not.

That was it. I snapped. I didn't scream or swear or argue. I just took his pitiful toothbrush and boiled it until the handle curled up and all the bristles stuck out in every direction. Calmly, I strode into the bedroom and handed it to him. Then walked out.

And thus, all unnecessary honey-do-thises and honey-do-thats came to a ceremonial end.

No Greater Love

Not until I became a mother did I realize something of great importance. I didn't have a personal relationship with Jesus Christ. I hadn't even realized that he wanted it.

I had great faith. I had sound doctrine. I believed Jesus was God's son, born of a virgin, and that he'd suffered death by crucifixion for my sins. I knew he was buried in a tomb, rose from the dead on the third day, and ascended into heaven.

Our family ate, drank, and worshiped, the Lutheran way. We had three ordained Missouri-Synod pastors in our family. I regularly took holy communion, so I figured I must be good with God.

But he wasn't just a part of the triune God—Father, Son, and Holy Ghost. He was *my* savior! And here's the part that finally hit home and changed everything: He was my friend.

"What a Friend We Have in Jesus" had always been a favorite hymn of Helen's as well as my Aunt Lou. But now it took on new meaning. The God of the universe was available to me morning, noon, and night. He was always happy to hear from me, Chrissy Emi. Not because I was anybody special, but simply because he loved me.

When the day came that this truth settled over my heart, I cried tears of joy.

Lord, I can really say anything to you, and it'll be okay? I can be angry, sad, pathetic, lazy, disappointed, scared, hopeless, or depressed? Any emotion is safe? Is there any way I could mess up that would make you stop loving me?

Jesus said, "Greater love has no one than this, that someone lay down his life for his friends" (John 15:13). I could honestly look into my little Mary's face and know this was now true for me. I would sacrifice anything for her. Yes, I would even lay down my life.

No one could have prepared me for the overwhelming sense of pure love that wrapped me and my baby like a great warm blanket of joy, contentment, and peace. No matter what anyone had tried to tell me, I could not fully appreciate the depth and weight and preciousness of this kind of love until I become a mother.

And this was the way God loved *me*? Could it truly be? Oh, how I needed this now, as I bumbled my way through motherhood.

Oh, Father! Now I understand what it means that your love is unconditional. You are a just God. Yet you choose to love and forgive me. I don't have to earn your love.

Another revelation followed, this one excruciating. As much as I had felt loved by my parents, and I had, it wasn't what

I'd call unconditional. It seemed to me that expectations had always been attached to their affections. Guidelines for acceptable performance. Somewhere I'd picked up a heavy burden of not wanting to disappoint them, and I carried it still. Both of my parents were quite intelligent and successful, and their high standards followed me around like a shadow.

Who knows why we human beings sometimes say or do things that have the potential to be grievously misunderstood. Once, when I was a young adult, my folks said something to me that affirmed my every childhood insecurity. "Chrissy," they said, "if you cross this particular line in the sand, we will disown you."

Ouch.

I gave this some thought before forming a response. In as respectful at tone as I could, I said, "May I ask one question? How many times in my life can I be disowned?"

In one careless sentence, my parents, the ones who had chosen me for adoption into their family, were willing to see me forever anchor my worth in their standards of behavior. Their version of my story said I was lovable, but with conditions.

Yet now I saw that God had always offered me a different story. His view said that my value, my belovedness, was inherent from the moment I was born. In fact, he proclaimed me priceless long *before* I was born.

Just as I had Mary. Aha!

The Lord had graciously let me be a mom, and I was going to love my children *His* way. I may not always like what they do or say. I may be disappointed or even hurt by some of their choices and outcomes. But my children would never doubt they'd still be loved. They'd be forgiven. This was the kind of love Jesus offered me.

The kind of love He offers us.

I was twenty-three years old, savoring the moment I'd been waiting for my whole life. My daughter, Mary, was beautiful. Sometimes I would scoop her up and swing her around, and we would dance and dance and dance. How she would laugh!

Tom loved to hold Mary up to his face and kiss her tiny nose. She would look at him, and her tiny fingers would fold together. We were a happy threesome, and life was good.

Thank you, Jesus! Help me be the kind of mother you created me to be.

> *What a friend we have in Jesus,*
> *all our sins and griefs to bear.*
> *What a privilege to carry*
> *everything to God in prayer!*
> *Can we find a friend so faithful*
> *who will all our sorrows share?*
> *Jesus knows our every weakness.*
> *Take it to the Lord in prayer.*[4]

6

A SHIFTING WIND

I will instruct you and teach you in the way you should go; I will counsel you and watch over you.

Psalm 32:8

And so it had begun that through my journey as a mother, Jesus would teach me to lean on Him, believing His plans were trustworthy and good.

Even when they looked very different from mine.

As the first weeks turned into months, we were having a sweet time. Tom healed and returned to making his long work commute to Los Angeles. When home, he loved to kiss Mary's little nose and nap with her. Meanwhile, Mary and I made regular outings to Puente Hills Mall. I even gave the ladies at The Children's Place my phone number, and they'd call whenever a new item arrived they thought Mary would look cute in. Of course, that was nearly everything.

In fact, Mary was so adorable, a photographer suggested I get her an agent so she could be on television. I approached this with caution, not wanting her to be exploited. One day an agent phoned. "There's a new burger place coming to southern California," he said. "They're looking for cute children for a commercial. Why don't you bring Mary down and we'll see how it goes?"

"What's the name of the burger place?" I asked.

"Wendy's."

I was skeptical. "Never heard of them, and I am not sure I want to bring Mary to this audition."

When he finally convinced me they were the real deal, I put Mary in the navy polka-dot dress Grandma Helen had found at Luan's and headed to the shoot. Mary easily won over their panel of judges. They asked me to put her in a high chair and get her to wipe her mouth with a napkin.

Oh dear. This was going to be a problem.

Breastfeeding had been such a win-win for Mary and me, we had never stopped. Her food supply was always handy, always at the right temperature, with no mess or fuss. My figure had never been better. Sadly though, I wasn't the only one who was thin. Mary's pediatrician wanted her to put on weight. "Start feeding her solids. She needs to eat!" he said.

As a first-time mom, I hadn't seen this coming. And the trouble was, Mary did not like sitting in her high chair and she rejected solid food. At home, I paid the two little kids who lived next door a quarter each to be silly and distract her, while I tried to get some food down the hatch. Even this didn't work very well, but, hey, we all had fun.

However, now, without the kids, Mary had no chance of pleasing the director of the Wendy's commercial. And thus ended her fifteen minutes of fame.

When Mary was fifteen months old, the pediatrician insisted I stop breastfeeding her altogether. Oh, the heartbreak. But by now she'd begun to take a sippy cup and sample solid foods. She slept through the nights and approached each day with enthusiasm. She was happy and energetic. She could walk, and she could run.

So Grandma Helen figured now would be a super time for Tom and me to finally get away. She generously made reservations for the two of us at the Disneyland Hotel for two nights and three days and rolled out the red carpet for Mary's visit.

Despite my fear that Mary wouldn't eat and drink enough for Helen and Paul, they all did just fine. Me, on the other hand? Not so good.

What had I been thinking? I'd just quit breastfeeding six or seven times a day, and I expected to be lounging poolside and riding the Matterhorn? How naive. A Jerseymaid cow doesn't exactly dry up overnight. I was in terrible pain. Tom spent his time running back and forth to the ice machine and packing me from waist to neck.

This wasn't Disneyland. This was hell.

Still more unforeseen changes were on the way.

As much as we loved our house and our neighborhood, I felt a strange, strong pull to move back to our old hometown. We were still spending a great deal of our time there, especially on Sundays when we would attend two church services in Long Beach—one at the Nazarene Church with Helen and Paul, and one at my family's church, Bethany Lutheran. What a joy to worship with family. And before heading home, we'd stick around for brunch or dinner.

Also on the plus side, Tom's work commute would shorten considerably if we moved back.

And then there was the spider issue. It makes me queasy even to recall it, but I'll push through and relate the gory details. In order to build our neighborhood, excavators had made deep cuts in a hill. This upset the balance of nature, I was told, although the science behind it was all very mysterious to me. What I knew for certain was that Mary was now crawling around and in daily danger of running into poisonous spiders.

Black widow cobwebs regularly adorned the inside of our attached garage, where I did the laundry. Our neighbor Gary told us how a black widow had reared up on its legs and chased him. He had to whack it three times with a shovel to kill it.

Once, while pushing Mary in a stroller down the street, a tarantula decided to accompany us.

Since we didn't have automatic garage door openers, opening and closing the door was a hands-on, life-or-death operation. One day, I slid the door open to find three enormous tarantulas there to welcome me. Screaming, I grabbed Mary from the car and tried to calm down while Tom ran for the shovel.

Arachnophobia is no joke, and I'd been bitten by it. Every day, paranoia threatened my sanity. "I cannot remain in this house any longer," I finally said. "We need to move back to Long Beach, the sooner the better."

But could we really say goodbye to our neighbors, to our yard, to the trees Tom planted that changed colors in fall? With Dad and Dave and Tom's help, we had just poured a slab in the backyard for a patio and barbecue area. We'd even inserted little Mary's feet and hands into the drying cement to personalize it.

Yet the urge to leave was overwhelming. Looking back later, I was convinced God had leveraged those creepy critters to draw us back to Long Beach. Unbeknownst to us, our proximity to medical help would soon become our new matter of life or death.

And we were going to need all the help we could get from family and close friends.

By the end of 1976, we'd settled into a darling little house just down the street from the high school where Tom and I met. We had three bedrooms, two baths, a tiny step-down den, and only a one-mile drive to either set of grandparents. Tom erected a swing set in the backyard. We were home.

The following May brought happy news. We had another baby on the way! My sister, Liz, had also started having babies. Mary loved playing with her cousin Tina, and now she was thrilled she'd soon be a big sister.

The presence of children was changing our family's dynamics, adding such delight. My cousin Alicia was now expecting her first baby, as was my friend Gloria. Let the good times roll, we all said, as we savored every moment of those exciting, carefree days.

A Gift Imparted

I am your servant; give me understanding, that I may know your testimonies!

Psalm 119:125

I felt good, if a little tired. Nothing that was unusual for a first trimester of pregnancy. I even took a job as a bank teller, so Tom could get a break from working two jobs. But something was different.

A sense of necessity and an air of awe encircled our lives. It started slowly, months before Sarah was born. It began with a whisper heard only by me.

This child you are carrying will have problems and many needs. But do not fear. I will walk with you and supply everything necessary.

Was I going crazy? Is that you, Lord?

Her life will glorify me.

Was the TV on? Or had God just spoken to me?

I tried to talk to Tom and my obstetrician, Dr. Meals, about what I had heard. "Our child is going to have complications," I said. But they wouldn't believe me. So I spoke of it no more. I just held the words close to my heart.

In 1 Kings 3:9 (MSG), Solomon asked the Lord for "a God-listening heart so I can lead your people well, discerning the difference between good and evil." I was beginning to recognize that God had given me a gift of discernment, a special kind of understanding I could call on, especially when I needed to distinguish between good and bad, light and darkness.

In this case, I knew in my spirit that what I heard was not the enemy whispering fears over me. Nor was it, to quote Ebenezer Scrooge, "an undigested bit of beef" or a "fragment of underdone potato."[5]

No, the Lord was giving me a prophetic heads-up.

In this place that required new levels of trust, I felt the rubber hitting the road. Was my Jesus nothing more than that one-dimensional cutout on the felt board in the church of my childhood? Or was he alive and real to me? Was he present? Approachable? Trustworthy?

Reality check. What good father doesn't speak to his children? Didn't Jesus tell us he communicates in ways we can hear? "My sheep hear my voice, and I know them, and they follow me" (John 10:27).

Are we not promised guidance, according to his wisdom? "In all your ways submit to him, and he will make your paths straight" (Proverbs 3:6 NIV). If I wanted the Lord to direct me, I would need to maintain a posture of surrender.

I've discovered something special about the word *heart*. Within it are the words *hear*, *ear*, and *art*. When we choose to tune into the Father with our whole hearts, with ears to hear, we become a work of art!

Lord, I don't know where you're taking me. But I feel you and I hear you, maybe for the first time in my life. You truly speak to me. I don't need my experience validated by anyone else. I'm listening. I choose to trust.

I've been accused more than once of having too-high expectations. Some have cautioned that I'd be wise to lower them, so I don't face disappointment. They make a good point. But know this about me: I have a platinum Hallmark membership card and I'm not afraid to use it.

I love life. I take it, grab it, smell it, taste and feel it. I believe in laughing out loud as often as possible and crying whenever something touches my heart. I smile when letters arrive in the mail and tear up at poignant commercials.

I do not want a lukewarm heart, even if it means sometimes getting hurt.

Even as Dr. Meals patted me on the hand and continued to reassure me that my pregnancy was progressing normally, I prepared for what was coming. God was in control, and his plans would prevail. Having foreknowledge allowed me to lay an emotional foundation.

Countless lives were about to be altered—some, forever. Some of us would be undone and rebuilt. Many would be made stronger.

7

A DELICATE SPARROW

⟶

For God gave us a spirit not of fear but of power and love and self-control.

2 Timothy 1:7

Could there possibly be a happier color than yellow? Not to my mind. So when it came to decorating the baby's room, this Hallmark girl didn't hold back. It would be bright, and it would be cheery, to welcome our new addition.

To complement the rich hunter-green carpet, we added buttercream wallpaper and curtains the color of soft sunshine. We set up the dark-oak baby furniture that had been Mary's, and at Christmastime, Grandma Helen added a stunning new handmade quilt. She also stitched a new picture to hang in the nursery. This one had a sparrow, and words that would prove to be quite prophetic.

"His eyes are on the sparrow."

At the same time, Mary, who would be three years old when the baby was born, got a room makeover. Tom hung Holly Hobbie wallpaper and painted the trim a crisp white. Grandma Helen and Grandpa Paul purchased a new, white bedroom set. Then we layered on a lovely, feminine bedspread and matching curtains, with tiny butterflies on a white background, and draped sheer fabric over the canopy of her new double bed.

The outside of the house received a fresh coat of paint also— yellow, with white shutters. It was quite a little dollhouse! My favorite thing in our garden was a trellis with yellow roses vining over it. My dad and Tom collaborated on building an adorable little yellow playhouse in the backyard. Of course, it too had white shutters, and even a Dutch door.

Then it happened. On a rainy night in February of 1978, Sarah Elisabeth came into our world.

Alone in the darkness of my hospital room, I watched the city lights go out one by one. Morning broke silently over a shiny, wet world. *Oh, please, let it have all been a bad dream!* I wanted to be back home in my own bed, watching Mary's delighted face as the baby moved and kicked inside me.

But when I moved my hand to my belly, my stomach felt flatter. As this new day was dawning, I couldn't escape my new reality. My mind replayed the events of the last hours, trying to make sense of everything that happened.

There had been so much rain.

When Tom came home and climbed into bed after his swing shift, I awoke to a long, hard contraction. Once I caught my breath, I rolled over and told Tom I thought we ought to get to the hospital. "Just wait a while," he said. Soon he was snoring.

I got out of bed, put on my slippers and robe, and had to hold onto the bedpost for support through another hard contraction. "Tom, wake up!" I said. "This baby is coming now!"

Still he refused.

"Tom, I'm serious. We're about to find out what God meant when he told me this child would have problems."

He turned toward me in a huff. "Are you still on that? Why don't you just drop it? The hospital will just check you and send you home. You'll see." With that, he went back to sleep. In fairness, Tom was exhausted, and my labor with Mary had been long.

But as a woman, you know these things.

God must have a great sense of humor. Better than mine sometimes. Out into the rain I went with my purse and keys in hand. I tried to open the driver's side door, but it was jammed, again. *You have got to be kidding me!* I circled the car, entered by the passenger door, lumbered over the stick shift of our little four-speed sedan, and drove myself to the hospital. *Okay, Lord, you said you would be with me and this child. I sure hope you're with us now, because it's 2:30 in the morning. I'm alone, soaking wet, cold, and in heavy labor. Please give me green lights all the way.*

Without a single red light to slow me down, I made it to Long Beach Community Hospital in ten minutes. *Thank you, Lord!* As I waddled inside, a woman jumped up and ran for a wheelchair. She wheeled me right past a room where my cousin Alicia was also laboring. Oh, that's right. Alicia and her husband, Kim, had paid Mary and me a visit earlier in the day, excited to tell me she was experiencing early signs of labor. We'd prayed together.

Kim spotted me and made a lot of fuss. "Chrissy, what are you doing here? Oh, wow, our children are going to have the same birthday!"

But at my stage of labor, I couldn't carry on a conversation. I just smiled tightly and waved to Alicia, who was pacing the room, her two ponytails swinging.

When the nurse discovered I was already dilated to eight centimeters, she called my obstetrician, Dr. Meals. Meanwhile, I tried to distract myself. I focused on the photo of Mary I'd brought with me. I repeated Psalm 23 over and over, like a chant. "The Lord is my shepherd; I shall not want. He makes me lie down in green pastures . . ."

In walked my cousin Kim, wide-eyed, with ice chips and massage lotion, ready to be of service. Evidently, Alicia was only dilated to two.

"Press hard on my lower back," I said.

"Where's Tom?"

I was already in transition, trying not to push. "Home sleeping, I guess. Harder. Press harder."

Kim flew out of the room to find a pay phone and wake Tom up. He must have put the fear of God in my husband, who still had to call his parents, wake up and deliver Mary to their house, and hightail it to the hospital. Somehow, Tom made it just as I was rolled into the delivery room.

Dr. Meals appeared in time for deliver Sarah's delivery, which was only thirty minutes after I arrived at the hospital. Just like with Mary, this baby came naturally, with no medications or other interventions.

"You have another girl," he said. "And she has a problem."

Oh, but for the saving grace of God, preparing me with this news beforehand! I had no idea what to expect, but at least I wasn't caught totally off guard.

There was a hole in her back, he explained. *Okay, this isn't so bad,* I thought. *They'll just graft some skin from me and patch her up. Then we can take her home and get on with our life. Right?*

Wrong. This wasn't a simple hole. The doctor called it a *myelomeningocele,* also known as *spina bifida.* Having never heard these terms before, I didn't know what any of it meant. But I would learn quickly.

When Tom saw little Sarah's back, he burst into tears. "It looks like a hand grenade blew up her back," he sobbed. Tom and I were both encouraged to rest, as there wasn't anything immediate to be done.

So Tom had left. And now here I lay, watching the city wake up, feeling like I was in the middle of some weird nightmare. A little at a time, I began to assimilate all the information my wonderful pediatrician had tried to convey. I drew on every ounce of strength I could find to break out of my haze. And now that I had, I realized what was at stake.

Oh, dear God, give me the strength, the wisdom, and the gumption to help Sarah! And by the way, she is so pretty. Thank you for my daughter!

What should I do next? I called both sets of grandparents and tried to be informative. Then I reached for the buzzer to call the nurse. "I want to see my pediatrician again, please."

Dr. Krueger returned quickly.

"Are Sarah's legs moving?"

"No," he replied. He informed me that because this hospital didn't have a Neonatal Intensive Care Nursery (NICN), he was coordinating with Miller Children's Hospital. An ambulance was on its way to transport Sarah.

I tried to remain calm. "When is the ambulance coming?"

"In just a few minutes. They are sending a specialist to ride with her."

My mind raced. "Shall I have her baptized before she goes in the ambulance?"

He thought a minute. "It's up to you," he said. "But she is stable, and her vital signs are good."

Tom returned just as the ambulance personnel were preparing Sarah for her trip. My mom, who had worked as a NICU nurse before, arrived also, offering to go with Tom to Miller to listen to what the specialist had to say and help translate the medical terminology. It wasn't easy for her to take off her grandma hat and put on her professional one.

As personnel filed in, filling my hospital room, I stroked Sarah's sweet little body through the holes in the side of the incubator. Now I was surrounded by the doctor, the specialist, two ambulance personnel, Tom, my mom, and the nurse who would be taking care of Sarah.

"What is your daughter's name?" the nurse asked in a soft, kind voice.

I turned to look at her through my tears. "Sarah is her name. Sarah Elisabeth."

She introduced herself. "I'll make a cute little sign for her crib, so everyone can call her by her name."

At that moment, this tiny kindness meant the world to me. I was flooded with warmth and appreciation.

When Tom and I chose her name, we had no idea what was in store for Sarah. It could not have fit her better. Sarah means "God's princess." Isaiah 60:2 is a Scripture associated with her name: "The Lord will arise upon you, and his glory will be seen upon you."

Sarah's entourage escorted her out, leaving me alone to reflect on all the unknowns. What would this adventure our family was embarking on look like? I prayed for God to ease my anxiety.

Beyond my door, I spotted a nurse wheeling a newborn in a crib. The baby had a shock of red hair. I laughed out loud, knowing it had to be my cousins' baby, as Kim was a redhead. Prayers answered; I'd been asking God to give them a safe delivery. But I agonized over how to tell them about Sarah's complications, and the tsunami it would set in motion. I especially didn't want my situation to create any awkwardness that might keep them from fully enjoying the special thrill of having a new baby in their arms.

My phone rang. It was Alicia, and she sounded so happy. I jumped right in to offer my congratulations. "I just saw a beautiful strawberry being wheeled past my door, and I said to myself, That has to be Kim and Alicia's!" We laughed. She shared that her name was Jessica, and she weighed ten pounds. Their families were there with them, celebrating.

"Chrissy, what's going on? Did Tom make it for your delivery?"

"Yes," I said. "Tom made it for the delivery."

"What did *you* have, a boy or girl?"

"Well, Alicia, I had a seven-pound, six-ounce girl." I explained that she was on her way to Miller Children's hospital to meet with specialists. "Sarah has a birth defect called *spina bifida*. But she's stable, and, Alicia, she has beautiful green eyes! No need to worry or be distracted from your glorious celebration. I love you, and I'm so happy for you and Kim."

Alicia began crying. "Let's pray for little Sarah." Together we prayed over the phone. The next thing I knew, my room filled with Kim and Alicia's extended family members, all coming to pray with me. What a beautiful and sacred moment.

The wait was killing me. Soon my obstetrician stopped by, and I was so happy to see him. He was not only a great doctor but a talented professional singer. No, he never serenaded me during labor and delivery.

Dr. Meals pulled up a chair next to my bed and did something surprising. He started to cry. He felt terrible for me that Sarah's birth defect was so horrendous and severe. I was flabbergasted. What was it with the men in my life? I had tried to prepare him and Tom. Had they dismissed a message from God because the messenger was a woman?

"Okay, then," I said, "Will you do something to help me?"

"Yes," he said. "Anything."

"Get me out of this hospital. I need to be with Sarah."

He shook his head adamantly. "I couldn't possibly discharge you yet. You just gave birth a few hours ago. You need to rest."

"Either let me out, or I will leave AMA (Against Medical Advice). I've got to call my family and pastor and arrange for Sarah to be baptized today."

Dr. Meals caved. Soon I was in a car with my dad, sister, and brother, on our way to meet our pastor at the children's hospital.

How alert and healthy Sarah looked! From the waist up, she looked perfect and robust. Her lower extremities were all accounted for, but tiny in comparison to her upper half. She seemed to watch me with her pretty green eyes. As silly as it might sound, I swore she smiled at me too. It felt good to be with her. She and I had bonded through the pregnancy and God's personal message of reassurance, which was for both of us.

"Do not worry little one," I whispered. "Jesus is with us, and he promised we will have what we need."

My sister, Liz (short for Elisabeth), agreed to be Sarah's god-mother. We all gathered around the tiny incubator, watching Sarah be baptized.

I was feeling fairly positive until I noticed the demeanor of my mom and Tom. Tom hung his head, and my not-so-subtle mom looked like the Grim Reaper had landed on my head. They had met with the pediatric neurosurgeon, and he had painted a bleak picture.

After saying goodnight to Sarah, Tom and I headed home. Mary would spend another night with Grandma Helen and Grandpa Paul. Meanwhile, I was about to endure one of the longest nights of my life. Tom let me know we had to be back at the hospital by 7:00 a.m. to meet with the specialist. "And give him our decision."

"What decision?" I said.

"He said she will be extremely handicapped. Crippled. Her quality of life will be very poor. The specialist said we should let her die."

I was stunned. How could this be? I'd just left her. She was alert and beautiful.

As Tom went on, I could see that his heart was heavy. "The thing is, she would need lots of surgeries. She will never be potty-trained because her bowels and bladder control aren't working either."

"What do you mean, 'let her die'?"

"If we don't have the surgery to close up the giant hole in her back, she will get an infection called meningitis and die. The hospital would keep her comfortable but not treat the infection."

Then Tom dropped the final blow to my heart. "I think . . . I think we should let her die. Chrissy, I can't handle a crippled, retarded child."

I was horrified and outraged. Throughout that gut-wrenching night, we cried together and argued. I prayed, and remembered the voice I'd heard early in my pregnancy. *Do not fear. I will walk with you and supply everything necessary.*

I said to Tom, "I respect and appreciate how difficult this is for you. I also respect you telling me how you feel. You work hard to support us. I promise not to ask anything from you except to continue working, so I can be a full-time mom to Mary and Sarah and take care of all Sarah's medical appointments. Look, Tom, we moved to this sweet yellow house right in between both grandparents. We have lots of love and support. We can do this! God will help us. He promised!

"I want Sarah," I cried. "I want her to have the surgery."

I couldn't wait to see Sarah the next morning, to tell her I loved her and that she need not worry about a thing. With Jesus, we would be alright.

At the NICU, I put on a gown and scrubbed my hands and forearms, following the instructions on the wall over a giant sink. Nearby hung another sign.

> *God, grant me the serenity*
> *to accept the things I cannot change,*
> *the courage to change the things I can,*
> *and the wisdom to know the difference.*

I read it to myself. Then I read it again, out loud. I'd run into The Serenity Prayer off and on throughout my life but never paid it much mind. I associated it with people recovering from a drug or alcohol problem.

Suddenly I understood why it was hanging over the door to the NICU. I needed God to grant me the serenity to accept

Sarah's birth defect. I would need Him to help me change the things I could, such as the doctors' and Tom's opinion about what constituted quality of life. And I'd need great wisdom to know the difference.

Suddenly I felt stronger than I had my entire life. I could count on God to give me the courage and endurance and knowledge to persevere in this matter for as long as needed. I would never again be an uninformed, unopinionated person.

My little sparrow's life hung in the balance.

8

A Song of Hope

For where your treasure is, there will your heart be also.

Luke 12:34

I had never been in an intensive care nursery, nor had I personally known anyone with a critically ill baby. So as I walked the halls that morning, I was shocked at the number of babies that are *not* born healthy and bouncy and big. In the NICU, I was far from alone. Many other parents were experiencing the same kind of grief, pain, and fear.

When we met with the surgeon, I sensed that under his gruff exterior beat a soft, compassionate heart. Tom and I assured him we understood full well that our child would be disabled. "We want the surgery to close her back," I said. "We want Sarah.

"So use all the God-given talents and medical miracles you have at your fingertips, and let God do the rest. God gave my daughter to me this way, and I love and accept her just as she is. The Lord will provide whatever strength I need to see her through life. Respectfully, sir, as long as the name embroidered on your white coat does not say 'God,' I don't believe you have the right to pronounce a death sentence on our daughter."

The Lord had given Sarah to us, and the Lord would take her away whenever it met *His* timing.

God had also arranged for some remarkable people to intersect with us on this journey. One such individual was Dr. Bosu, another NICU specialist. Once we got Sarah's surgery scheduled, he approached me with a twinkle in his eyes. "I am so glad you have opted for life for Sarah. I was looking at her last night, after her arrival. She has a strong spirit! She will do well."

His confidence and delight were contagious. "You truly have a little angel on your hands," he mused. "God is at work, and you are trusting him. Oh, yes, Sarah will do well. She will touch many lives in many ways."

When Sarah's back was closed up, the spinal fluid that had been leaking through the hole in her spine went instead to her brain. She developed *hydrocephalus*. Her head would get very large, and a shunt was inserted with a straw-like tube attached. The shunt funneled off the fluid from the brain, sending it down the attached tubing that had been placed beneath her skin and into her stomach. Five more times, she required shunt revisions. Each time the shunt got plugged up, I manually pumped it as the doctors had taught me, in an attempt to unclog it. It was a flawed, manmade solution to a complex problem.

Sarah's doctors at least became enthusiastic. Not hopeful. There was a difference.

By the time Sarah came home from the hospital for the first time, she'd undergone two surgeries. Mary wasn't allowed in the NICU, so she hadn't yet been able to see or touch her baby sister. Although she was sweet and gentle, she was still too young to understand how fragile Sarah was. So Tom and I decided it was too risky to keep Sarah in the cradle. We could imagine Mary wanting to rock Sarah, and that might spell disaster. I did lay Sarah in the cradle once, just to be able to say to myself she had been in it.

Sarah did have some sensation below her waist, although the doctors disputed this fact. Due to the impaired mobility in her lower extremities, she had to have eight orthopedic surgeries to release muscles and tendons. So Sarah spent a lot of her life in casts.

After yet another of these surgeries, my gift of discernment came into play. Sarah was returned to her hospital crib with her leg in a cast, and the cast was wrapped in bandages. Sarah was not normally a screaming child, but she had come out of this surgery loud and upset.

I knew something was horribly wrong, but the nurse wouldn't listen. I warned her that if she didn't unwrap the bandage from Sarah's leg, I would. "You can't do that," she commanded. "She just had surgery on that leg!" When I started to unwrap it, she ran out, yelling, "I am calling the doctor right now. You are in so much trouble!"

I removed Sarah's bandages and pried open the cast that was sandwiched on her leg like a clamshell. Lo and behold, Sarah stopped crying. The cast had been pinching the outside of her calf, and the skin was red and inflamed. The doctor blew into the room looking ready to attack me. When he saw Sarah's angry red leg and the tracks of her tears, he apologized profusely. Carefully, he redressed the leg. "I will never again assume someone has no sensation," he said.

As a result of Sarah's many surgeries, Mary spent a lot of time with her grandparents. What a godsend that we all lived so close now, although Mary was always eager to reunite with her little sister at home. We were continually sustained by the devotion of our extended family and friends, always giving generously in a spirit of love, patience, and true understanding.

Sarah had such a lovely spirit, always smiling through her trials. She was our beautiful, shining angel, who just happened to have a physical flaw called spina bifida. She loved sunshine, the color yellow, and laughing. All of us laughed a lot. It seemed that God had never been more alive and present.

We were able to pull strength and fortitude from a layer deep inside ourselves we didn't know we had. People would often shake their heads and say to us, "Oh, no . . . I can't even imagine . . ." But we were only doing what we had to do. And God's grace never ran out.

Often I would rock Sarah, softly singing "Annie's Song" by John Denver, tears of gratitude flowing. It became our special song. *You fill up my senses . . .*

Sarah continued to surpass all the doctors' expectations. She was so full of life and enthusiasm; she was becoming our family's teacher. We kept gaining a greater and greater understanding of true joy. Loving her helped us reevaluate our priorities.

Tom was a committed and loving dad. He continued working the swing shift in Los Angeles and even took extra jobs on the weekends painting houses, so I was able to stay home. After Sarah was born, my dad started coming over every morning to play with the kids and help out. He bought me my first cast iron skillet, for making scrambled eggs and Pillsbury cinnamon rolls. He always let the girls have the leftover icing.

As Mary grew, so did her circle of friends. She loved playing "school" and roller-skating up and down our sidewalks with neighbors Dana and Lori, whose parents became good friends of ours. But she especially loved being a big sister to Sarah.

One day, because Tom was working swing shift, we had dinner for lunch and breakfast for dinner. While I was chatting with a friend on the kitchen phone, I realized I'd been hearing Sarah and Mary laughing loudly for a long time, and their laughter was getting more intense. "I'd better hang up and see what those girls are up to," I told my friend.

I followed the sound of laughter to Sarah's bedroom and slowly pushed the door open to peek. I could hear a *crunch, crunch, crunch* and smelled the sweet aroma of Cheerios. I could not see the green carpet in Sarah's bedroom. Sarah was sitting in her crib, and Mary was standing inside the crib with a big box of Cheerios.

"What are you playing?" I asked. Mary stuck her hand inside the box, pulled out a handful, and threw them up in the air. Sarah laughed and clapped.

"Sarah has never seen snow," Mary said sweetly. "So I was pretending the cherries were snow!" I realized then that the green carpet was already "snow-covered," so I just sat down on the floor among the "snow cherries." The three of us had a "snow fight" until all the Cheerios were gone. I loved being a mother, and I loved my silly daughters!

Sarah developed *petit mal* seizure disorder. When a seizure would occur, she would stare out with a blank look on her face, turn grey, vomit, and then fall into a deep sleep. After her developmental physician, Dr. Geraldine Stramski, put her on a low dose of the anti-seizure medication phenobarbital, Sarah had only one seizure over the following year.

On July 17, 1979, when Sarah was seventeen months old, she suddenly became very ill. Her head was normal, with no frontal lobe swelling, and she didn't have projectible vomiting. I rushed her to Miller Children's Hospital. They had me bring her up to a treatment room, rather than the emergency room, and a neurosurgeon was paged.

The doctor asked, had she ever had spinal meningitis? "Thankfully, no," I said, recalling with terror how Sarah's first neurosurgeon had recommended leaving her back open and vulnerable to spinal meningitis. *So she would die.*

Oh, God, no! I was screaming in my head, as I watched him stick a needle into her spine to draw out spinal fluid for testing. "If the fluid drawn is not clear, we'll know she has meningitis." As I watched, the syringe filled up with a cloudy, dark fluid.

He immediately started barking orders. "Get Sarah into a room immediately! Start IV antibiotics. She must be in isolation." I was told to leave while they set her up in a different room.

I tore downstairs to the hospital chapel. "No, God, please!" I screamed. "Give us more time with Sarah. I am not ready to lose her!"

I ran back upstairs and put on a gown. One of the nurses was prepping Sarah's arm, getting ready to start the antibiotics. Suddenly a lab tech came running into the room waving a piece of paper in his hand. "What are you doing?" someone shouted. "You can't be in here without scrubbing. She's in isolation."

"No, listen!" the tech said. "She doesn't have meningitis. While we were running the test, her spinal fluid suddenly turned clear. We couldn't believe it. Don't start the antibiotics."

I looked at Sarah who had been so ill and lifeless. Her lovely green eyes were now open. She smiled at me and clapped her chubby little hands. The nurse took her temperature. It was normal. Soon the doctor came into the room and discharged us home.

Alrighty then, Sweetheart. Let's go home, and enjoy the good 'ole summertime. Is God real? Does He hear our prayers? Oh yes, He is, and yes, He does!

And we did enjoy a full summer. Mary and Sarah had a wonderful, amazing bond. Even though she spent a lot of time around Alicia's baby, Jessica, who was born only a few hours after Sarah, and my good friend Gloria's daughter Jennifer, who was three weeks older than Sarah, Mary had an instinct for understanding what Sarah could and could not do. She was Sarah's biggest fan, as well as her protector.

We discouraged Mary from picking Sarah up to move her, especially when Sarah was in casts. So when Sarah, seeing the other children running to play in our backyard, would point and said, "Outside please, Mary," Mary would come and grab Tom, or me, or one of the grandparents, to move Sarah outside. Then she'd sit with her arm around Sarah on the swing glider, making sure she never slid off.

One sunny southern California afternoon, I was hanging out clothes on our clothesline, which was perched in a hole in the middle of our driveway in the backyard. I liked to let the sun bleach and sterilize Sarah's cloth diapers. I parked Sarah's playpen in the shade and propped her in her yellow baby chair. At the time, she had a cast on each leg and a bar between her legs. I let down the side of the playpen, so she could watch us. Mary rode her tricycle in and out of the sheets for most of an hour, making Sarah laugh hysterically.

When I became a mother, I embraced life like never before. Butterflies. Disneyland. Sprinklers on a hot summer day. Donuts with sparkles. Whipped cream. Bubbles. Puppies. I love the purr of a kitten. But the best sound in the whole wide world is a child's pure, unrestricted laughter.

We often made a trip to Disneyland over Fourth of July weekend. The crowds never bothered us. That summer, we went twice. Double your pleasure, double your fun . . .

In the fall, we did another thing twice. We stayed at my cousin Janie's adorable mountain cabin. While Tom painted the exterior, the girls and I played in the fallen leaves. Once, as Sarah crawled outside on the ground, she picked up a big sliver under one of her fingernails. Tom put Sarah in his lap, and Mary stood by, holding her other hand. "It's okay, Sarah," she cooed, "Daddy will make it okay!" While Tom pulled out the sliver with tweezers, Sarah never even whimpered. Mary kissed Sarah's finger to make it all better.

On our second trip to the cabin, my pregnant sister, Liz, her husband, Ron, and their daughter, Tina, were able to join us. We had a blast, while Ron helped Tom get the painting finished up before the snow flew.

On Halloween, Sarah was in double casts up to her waist. So I got her a Casper the Friendly Ghost mask. I cut a hole in a white sheet, pulled it over her head, and added white tights on her legs. She loved it. She made herself giggle and giggle, lifting her arms up and down to make the sheet move. Mary was all decked out as a ballerina.

We set the two girls, the ghost and the ballerina, on the loveseat and began shooting a home movie. Sarah leaned forward, grabbed Mary's mask, pulled it out, and let it go. It all happened so fast; I couldn't rescue poor Mary. She cried, and we corrected Sarah for her inappropriate action. "Sorry, Mary," Sarah said. "I love you!"

Mary hugged her baby sister. "I forgive you, Sarah."

Sarah's bright, sunny spirit was contagious.

My life as a mom was full of meaning. And I had found my voice. I was no longer that people-pleasing, yes-ma'am, yes-sir girl without gumption. If I wasn't my children's protector and advocate, who would be?

One gorgeous day, I took Mary and Sarah to a local park. A funny thing happened there. While my girls played and giggled, a poem sprang into my heart, and I wrote it down.

The Seed of Love

The greatest gift we're given is to know that someone cares.
To feel love and to give love are the richest seeds we bear.
So let us plant the seed of love and nourish it with time,
until it weathers all the cold and ice of wintertime.
And watch it blossom in the spring and glow at autumn's tide,
for you're a very special seed, a seed that is all mine.
So sing a song of joy for all the children of today
and all the children everywhere who help to show the way
to make the most of living in each and every day.
Our children hold the key to life—God planned it just that way.
You are what God has made you, and he made you just for me,
to fulfill his special purpose in life's cycle of timeless dreams.
The children are the seed of love. The only difference is,
some seeds are planted under hearts and some begin within.
So sing a song of joy for all the children of today
and all the children everywhere who help to show the way
to make the most of living in each and every day.
The children hold the key to life—God planned it just that way.

9

A Time to Weep

It is the LORD your God who will go with you. He will
not leave you or forsake you.

Deuteronomy 31:6

Out of the blue, on Christmas Eve of 1979, Sarah
had a *petit mal* seizure during our family Christmas
gathering.

Dr. Stramski's response was to call for an increase in Sarah's phenobarbital dosage. Although I had total respect for Dr.
Stramski, I also had reservations. I was no doctor, but one seizure in a year didn't seem valid reason to increase such a heavy-
duty medication on our little Sarah. So we compromised. Dr.
Stramski agreed to run a drug therapeutic level test, to see how
effective the current dose was for Sarah's needs.

About a week into the new year, 1980, I took her to Miller
for the blood test. Dressed in her favorite blue overalls over a
long-sleeve red tee shirt, shoes, and her leg braces, Sarah lay on
her back as the lab tech directed. He rolled up her right sleeve,

positioned a tourniquet, and turned to me. "This is called a blood gas test. I have to go very deep, and it will be very painful."

I felt horrible for having to put Sarah through this. Guilty and scared. I berated myself silently. *Oh, great move, Mom, making her endure this awful test just because you don't want her to be overly drugged.* I considered telling the tech to stop the procedure.

He stuck the needle into her arm. She didn't even flinch. No tears. No crying.

I, on the other hand, had tears streaming down my cheeks. "I am so sorry, Sweetheart. You are so brave. I love you, Sarah."

Sarah lifted her free arm, reached up to my face, wiped my tears, and smiled. "Mom," she said, softly, lovingly. Like an angel, she bolstered my feeble spirit.

When the test results came in, Dr. Stramski phoned to report that the drug had registered as *low therapeutic* in her system. If Sarah had even one more seizure, she would be increasing the dosage.

A week later, on January 17, 1980, I took the girls shopping for decorations and party favors for Sarah's second birthday party, which was two weeks away. It was a cold winter day, threatening to rain. We met up with my good friend Kathy and her son Eric, and capped off the afternoon with lunch and fancy dishes of ice cream at Farrell's Ice Creme Parlour. When we got home, Mary and Sarah played together.

Before leaving for his swing shift, Tom set Sarah on his lap. He liked making her giggle by taking off his cap and putting it on her head. She liked pulling on his moustache. Tom kissed her goodbye.

The girls and I planned to have breakfast for dinner, our favorite, right after their bath. Bath time was fun time for those two, and we embarked on our nightly routine. I strapped Sarah into her little bath chair. Within our small home, I could always see or hear everything going on. After I'd listened to them splashing and playing for a while, I entered the bathroom. "Okay, girls, let's get out and have breakfast-for-dinner!"

"Okay, Mom," said Mary.

"Sarah, are you ready to get out?" I asked. She smiled at me and shook her head no. "Okay, I'll just put Mary's pajamas on and be right back for you, then we'll have dinner."

Mary's bedroom was right next door to the bathroom. I quickly dried Mary off and slipped on her long nightgown. When I returned to the bathroom, I was stunned to find Sarah somehow out of her bath chair. And she was floating. I scooped her right up, fully expecting her to start coughing or at least moving.

When she didn't, I worked to stay calm. I dialed 9-1-1 and also called my neighbor Kim, who lived across the street. I laid Sarah on the living room carpet to give her mouth-to-mouth resuscitation and noticed vomit in her mouth. I wiped it out with the fabric of my blue bathrobe. Mary stood next to me, crying. "Mommy, what's wrong with Sarah? Why doesn't she wake up?"

I asked her to run and fetch our neighbor Kim, who was a nurse. "But, Mommy," Mary cried, "it's dark, and I can't cross the street without help." Of course, she was right! I wasn't thinking straight. *Oh, dear God! Help me!*

Finally, the paramedics arrived. Although they weren't carrying a pediatric intubating tube in their kit, they began CPR. They could not give Sarah an airway.

Kim arrived, drained the tub, and took Mary to her home, grabbing my phone book on her way out. She called Tom, both sets of grandparents, and other family members. She also called our church.

I demanded to ride in the ambulance with Sarah. The crew wouldn't allow me in the back with her, so I settled for riding up front. When they hustled her into an emergency room, I refused to leave. The medical staff pointed to a small stool and demanded I sit by silently. One sound, they warned, and I would be out.

I watched. I prayed. I begged God for mercy. *Save Sarah, please God!*

How could this have happened? I was right there. This was our nightly routine. How had she gotten out of her bath chair? *Dear God, please, please save Sarah!*

"I am so sorry, but there is nothing we can do." I heard the ER doctor's somber words, and they didn't feel real. This wasn't possible.

"No!" I begged, my eyes and ears glued to the heart monitor. Every now and then I'd heard a *beep, beep*. "You must not give up! Sarah never quit. Please keep trying." I felt like a cheerleader, but this was not a game. This was life and death. My daughter's.

Sarah and I were a team. Together, *we* had been through it all. The fourteen surgeries in twenty-three months, the rehabilitation four times a week, the braces, all of it. We were family, and we were better because of Sarah. She was our angel, God's princess. I could not and would not let her go.

I wavered between reality—seeing my bare, cold toes on the hospital floor, peeking out from under my long blue robe—and disbelief. *Dear God, no. Not now. Not ever. You can't take her from me.* So often I had almost expected to lose her. The spinal meningitis scares. The dangers involved with each of the six brain and eight orthopedic surgeries. *But not now, Lord!*

After nearly two hours had passed in the ER, I heard the doctor's voice again, "I'm truly so sorry," he said tearfully. "I have a little girl her age at home. But Sarah is gone."

"No, no, no," I chanted. A kind of horrified numbness had set in.

At some point, someone said, "You have a phone call from your pediatrician. You can take it right here on the wall." *Oh, God, I'm so ashamed. How can I speak to this doctor who has been so steadfast and supportive ever since Mary was born over four years ago?*

"I am so sorry, Chris." At the sound of Dr. Krueger's tender, non-judgmental voice, I dissolved into a puddle of tears. "This must be horrible for you. Please call me if you need anything at all. Anything."

The hospital staff left me there with instructions that I could touch Sarah, but I was not to move or lift her. This was a coroner's case, they said. I sat alone on my little stool staring at her lifeless body. Devastated.

Then I felt a hand rest heavily on my right shoulder. I turned, expecting to see my dad or possibly Tom. But no one was there. The weight of the hand on my shoulder bared down. Suddenly I was surrounded by light and warmth. I felt peace.

Before my eyes, blue skies appeared, and, very clearly, a white archway. Under the archway stood Jesus. He held Sarah's hand. Standing next to Jesus, Sarah smiled and waved at me. Standing. For the first time in her life, Sarah was . . . *standing*!

Jesus and Sarah smiled brightly at me, then waved goodbye. "Let her go, Chris," Jesus said. "Sarah is with me now."

Sarah was safe! She was home with Jesus. As soon as I let this reality sink in and accepted it, the weighted hand left my shoulder.

The room went cold and dark again, yet I felt aglow. This, this was the peace that passes all understanding. I'd felt the Lord's touch. I'd seen his glory. I'd given my sweet Sarah back to her Creator. To her heavenly Father.

My peace and reverie came to an abrupt halt, as two Long Beach police officers confronted me, leading me off to the side of the emergency room. Oh, duh! Alert to Chris! Your daughter just drowned at home while you were there. And you have another small child living in the home who they may believe is in danger too. *Dear God, help me through this.*

The officers remained calm and spoke gently. I had no choice but endure their barrage of questions.

> *Who was home?*
> *Why did you leave her alone in the tub?*
> *How long were you out of the room?*
> *Where is your other child right now?*
> *Did you hear anything—splashing, coughing, struggling?*

This was the question that troubled me most. Our home was so tiny. How had I heard nothing? *Oh, Lord. I'm a monster. A horrible, reckless pathetic mother who may face negligence charges. What if they take Mary from me?*

Despite my fear and self-loathing, despite Satan's accusatory voice, no charges were ever filed. Mary was never removed from our home.

The rain had stopped, and we drove in silence to Kim's to pick up Mary. Tom held Mary in his lap, as the three of us sat together on the curb across the street from our little yellow house. "Look up to the sky, Sugar," Tom said, pointing to the stars overhead. "Way up there is heaven, where Jesus is. Sarah is going to live with Jesus in his heavenly home now. She won't live in our house anymore. Jesus came and took her home tonight."

Mary looked to the sky thoughtfully, and then to her daddy and me. "Daddy, does Jesus have pajamas in heaven? Because Sarah went to heaven with no clothes on, and she will get cold."

I lost it. Mary was still the big sister, forever caring and protecting. Even I, Sarah's mother, had failed to accomplish that feat.

Everybody came over to our home, and Tom made coffee. The atmosphere felt like a wake, and I was not having any of it. I pounded my knuckles on the wall, climbed into Sarah's crib, screaming, "Why, God?" Then I became absolutely stir crazy and had to get out of the house.

Barefoot, I ran through the rain in my flannel nightgown. Tom followed me out into the dark, begging me to come in. I ignored him. Then I heard my dad's voice. "Let her go, Tom. She'll come back."

Early in the morning following that nightmarish night, the phone rang. I awoke, numb and confused. "Hello?" I answered.

From the other end came a gruff male voice. "Are you the mother of Sarah?"

Tears sprang to my eyes. "Yes. Who is this?"

"This is the Los Angeles Coroner's Office. I have your daughter on the slab, ready to begin her autopsy, and I am appalled by all the scars on her body!"

Oh, no you don't, I thought to myself, *You are not going to insinuate that I have been abusing and my daughter!* I mustered the strongest voice I could. "Look, sir. Where do you want to start—at her head, or at her toes? Right here, right now. Come on, let's go. I can tell you what every scar is, I can give you the date of all fourteen surgeries. I will supply the physicians' names who performed the surgeries, and why she had them."

I raked that coroner over the coals. After listening to my litany of surgeries, dates, and outcomes, he apologized for being so suspicious. But I hung up feeling sick to my stomach, picturing Sarah's precious body, with her sweet, chubby little hands, laying still on his cold slab like a piece of meat.

Tom and I went to the mortuary on the following Sunday. As the mortician wheeled Sarah into the viewing room in her little pink casket, she said, "I thought this was a coroner's case."

"It is a coroner's case. Why?" I asked.

"In all my years as a mortician, I have never seen a coroner *not* perform an autopsy when it's a coroner's case."

I was stunned. Tears of joy and gratitude pressed. "Are you serious?"

"No one has touched her little body. I just dressed her in the dress you brought and did her hair. She sure has a beautiful head of hair."

I smiled, so relieved that Sarah had not had an autopsy after all. "That's because she had six brain surgeries for shunt revisions. Each time, they shaved her head. And each time her hair grew in more full and luscious."

Tom and I sat there with her all day, flabbergasted by how many people came by to pay their respects to our little angel.

The church was packed for her funeral. I went through the emotions, but inside I felt numb. When Sandy, Sarah's physical therapist, and Dr. Krueger approached the small pink casket, I became choked with emotion. These two individuals had been my link to all of Sarah's care and progress.

As friends of my cousin Alicia began playing the guitar and singing "Annie's Song," I sobbed quietly. This had been our song, the one that captured how being Sarah's mom made me feel. In his message, Pastor Loesch beautifully conveyed Sarah's essence and her zeal for life. The way she had done everything "with her whole heart."

After the graveside gathering, everyone left except Dad and me. Tom was waiting in our car. Sarah's pink casket had not yet been lowered into the ground. I insisted Dad leave, but he said, "I am not leaving until you and Tom have driven away. I know you, Chrissy Emi. You will jump into the grave with Sarah."

For the next six months, I visited the cemetery every day. Poor, sweet Mary. I had no choice but to drag her along with me. I tended Sarah's flowers and polished her beautiful headstone. Among the lambs and the cherub engraved on Sarah's headstone were these words:

Sarah Elisabeth

born 2-4-1978

died 1-17-1980

God's Princess

Isaiah 60:2 The LORD shall arise upon thee
and his glory shall be seen upon thee.

Just as God had promised early in my pregnancy, Sarah's life had always been meant for his glory.

For a long time, I continued wrestling with grief and self-disdain. I struggled to forgive myself. Did I let Sarah and Mary play in the bathtub? Yes, when her casts were off, and she was strapped into her bath chair. Should I have left them alone to play? No. In hindsight, I shouldn't have. Hindsight can be so cruel.

Remarkably, Tom never once blamed me for Sarah's death. What a grace.

Daily, I focused on Mary and shut the rest of the world out. In an effort to find some kind of closure, I went on a quest for answers. So many questions still lingered.

I went to the fire department that had responded to my 9-1-1 call. They confirmed that Sarah had still been alive when they arrived, but unfortunately, they had not had the ideal intubating tube. Normally they carried one, but for some reason not that day.

I visited the emergency room doctor who worked for over two hours to save Sarah's life. He reviewed the records with me, confirming that it would have been helpful if the paramedics had gotten a good airway started. But, he added, in his heart he believed that even if he had been able to stabilize Sarah, she would have been left with profound brain damage. Likely, she would have been on a ventilator for life. He also mentioned that he too had seen vomit in her mouth.

A light bulb suddenly went on. "Since we know she had vomited, and she was not sick with a flu, and her shunt was working, so there'd been no projectile vomiting, and since I heard no splashing or noise . . . Doctor, could Sarah have had one of her *petit mal* seizures? She would have silently gone into a blank stare, vomited, and then fallen forward, snapping the bath-chair strap. Could that be why I didn't hear a sound?"

"That makes perfect sense," the doctor said. "I was wondering how she had entered such a deep state of unconsciousness within just a couple of minutes."

Perhaps the "one more seizure" Dr. Stramski had worried about had come to pass on January 17, 1980, while Sarah played in the tub. I will never know for sure. But my calm detective work did help me obtain a level of understanding that hadn't been possible when my adrenaline was pumping. The dust had settled, and this tiny bit of clarity eased my emotional distress.

What I had the most clarity and confidence about was that Jesus called Sarah home. She was healthy and whole at last.

Also, if I could personally handle anything that came my way, why would I need God? Jesus Christ knew my world was going to feel cold and cruel. Yet his love and comfort broke through. He'd been present right in the middle of it all.

C. S. Lewis wrote, "Pain insists upon being attended to. God whispers to us in our pleasures, speaks in our consciences, but shouts in our pain. It is His megaphone to rouse a deaf world."[6]

And I was hanging on His every word.

10

A Grief Redeemed

This is my comfort in my affliction, that your promise gives me life.

Psalm 119:50

A month after Sarah's death, we got a kitten for Mary, thinking a furry companion might help her through her grief. She named it Tinkerbelle.

One Saturday, I decided to brave life and attempt some grocery shopping at Lucky's. When I left, all was calm on the home front. Tom was outside doing yardwork. Mary was playing with her new kitten.

When I returned an hour later, everything was turned upside down—and wacky, but not in a funny way. I entered the kitchen to find Mary seated at our little round table, crying. Tom stood nearby looking angry and annoyed.

"What the heck happened since I left?" I said.

"You know that kid up the street who likes to race his big, old stupid truck up and down the street?" Tom barked. "Mary crossed the street to visit Dana. All of a sudden, here comes that kid. And at the same time, Tinkerbelle runs after Mary and gets squished."

Since Mary hadn't seen it happen, Tom explained, he quickly ran into the street with a shovel and buried the kitty behind our garage. "Mary just got home, and I told her Tinkerbelle is gone."

Oh, dear God in heaven, help us!

Later, I would wonder what possessed me to respond the way I did. If I had it to do over, I might let things slide. But oh, no, not that day. I was indignant and I was upset. I was on a mission! By golly, I thought, this is the perfect opportunity to teach Mary about death.

"Dig it up, Tom. We're going to have a funeral."

He looked at me like I had flipped my lid. Maybe I had. "No way," he said. "I am not digging up a dead cat." We kept our tense voices hushed, for Mary's sake.

"Either you dig it up, or I will!" I called the grandparents and neighbors to come over and participate in a memorial service for Tinkerbelle. Then Mary and I went in search of her kitty's favorite toys and blanket. Meanwhile, Tom dug up the kitten and cleaned off its gray and white fur.

Mary wrapped Tinkerbelle and her toys in a little blanket and tucked her in the hole in the ground. Tom gave me a look that communicated he wouldn't mind smashing my head with the shovel. But instead, he set the shovel down and comforted Mary, saying some sweet parting words about the little kitty. Our neighbor Kim had to pinch herself to keep from laughing. I guess we all needed a little comic relief after the intensity of the past weeks.

After we said a prayer and thanked Tinkerbelle for blessing our family for a short while, we sang "Jesus Loves Me." Mary was no longer crying and seemed to have some closure. She returned to Kim and Dana's house to play. I thanked Tom for cooperating and apologized for possibly pushing him past the point of all that is right and decent.

Often, over the course of the following months, while Mary played in the backyard or at the beach, I read books by Elisabeth Kübler-Ross, who was an esteemed psychiatrist renowned for her work with dying children.

I was a real fun mom.

One afternoon, while strolling along the shore of Mother's Beach, Mary and I ran into a friend from church. She and her daughter were also out enjoying the day. "So, how are you doing after losing Sarah?" she asked.

"I'm still numb," I said. "I'm just focusing on Mary."

"Well, I sure hope you are not having any more babies!"

I've always admired women who are able to speak their minds, but this felt like a slap. *Just move on, Chrissy. Let it go.*

Over summer, we traveled to Yosemite with Helen and Paul in a huge, rented RV. Our adventure went pretty well—if you don't count the time Paul backed the rig over our row of bicycles, mowing them down. Or when I tried to help Helen with dinner by rinsing out the fresh spinach. Evidently, I wasn't thorough. After taking a bite, Paul was spitting out dirt. We all looked at each other and busted out laughing.

Fall arrived. Rather than attempting a traditional Thanksgiving celebration with family, Tom and I opted to rent a cabin in Big Bear with some friends of ours from Rowland Heights, Rene and Jim. Their son, Stevie was around Mary's age. Spontaneously, we all made a trip to Santa's Village, which in those days was quite a tourist attraction. At Christmastime, there was snow and even live reindeer.

Snow was falling sideways on that cold day, so we had Mary and Stevie all bundled up. We hung together, trying to stay warm while we waited in a long line so the kids could see Santa. As we got closer to Santa's house, I peeked through the window. "Hey," I said to our little group, "this Santa really looks like the real deal! Check him out." Everyone agreed that yep, if Santa were real, this guy could be him.

At last, our turn came. Stevie scampered up onto Santa's lap. After receiving his candy cane, he slid down. Now Mary climbed onto Santa's lap. The rest of us stood close by. "Well, now, Mary, I am sure you are missing Sarah this Christmas." Mary nodded her head. "Don't you worry. She is happy, and she wants you to have a happy Christmas too!"

Mary just looked at him like it was the most natural thing in the world to have Santa speak about Sarah. The four of us adults looked at each other in total shock. Jim and Tom had to excuse themselves and walk outside. Rene and I joined them. While Mary and Stevie played on some little elf statues, the grownups cried together, exclaiming about this miracle we had all witnessed. "Are you kidding?" we said. "That was the most wonderful but shocking thing I have ever heard or seen!"

I never mentioned to the others that Santa had also winked at me. The miracle was enough, and we all accepted it as just that. A Christmastime miracle.

I'd been feeling different physically. Could it be? Indeed, another miracle was in the making. I'd prayed for another child, and now we were again expecting. Not everyone seemed ready to rejoice with us. Fear is a natural human response.

I noticed that Mary's excitement too was somewhat guarded. But she loved to touch my growing belly and talk to her new sibling.

Once again, we decided not to learn the sex of the baby. A harder decision was choosing whether or not to test for birth defects. Would this baby be healthy and perfect? Sometimes my friend's careless words on the beach that day haunted me. But I clung to the truth that, boy or girl, with or without health complications, God would again provide all that was needed.

When our children touch a hot stove and get burned, they learn to stay away from the stove. Similarly, although the idea of having another baby was delightful in my heart, Tom was scared. And he wasn't alone.

So to put family at ease, I agreed that I would have an amniocentesis test at the appointed time in my pregnancy. To conduct this test, the doctor inserts a needle into the uterus and draws out some amniotic fluid. The test is great for detecting chromosomal abnormalities such as Down syndrome, but at the time was less conclusive for detecting spina bifida. During the same visit, an ultrasound would be administered, which would likely reveal any abnormalities of the baby's spine.

The Christmas season arrived, bittersweet. Unboxing Christmas decorations and Advent calendars with both Mary's and Sarah's names on them took my breath away. Over the years, I had accumulated many angel ornaments, so I decided this was the year I'd start an angel-themed tree.

Helen and Paul surprised us with a new piano. I was flabbergasted. I loved to play, and I looked forward to giving Mary and the new baby piano lessons if they wanted to learn. Mary and I plunked on the keys together and laughed. I sensed that our house would be filled with music and singing. And whenever Dad came over, we could now play duets.

Joy was beginning to spring up in our home again. I was no longer feeling the need to go to the cemetery all the time.

Mary was now a very active kindergartener at Bethany Lutheran school. Key words: *very active.* Her teacher was a wonderful, Christ-filled woman named Allysia. Having no shortage of energy, Mary had trouble understanding why Allysia asked the kids to put their heads down and rest while she played music on a record player. Mary, of course preferred to jump up and dance. As Mary's proud mom, it wasn't easy to watch the children pour out of class every day with a gold sticker for good behavior, while Mary often exited the room with none. She worked hard, she loved school, and she often earned gold stickers. But not every day.

Already, Mary was an old soul. She had been through so much for her young age. She was a survivor. And there were many days when my heart was in a twist, wishing she hadn't endured so much pain and loss.

The months of pregnancy passed, and the time arrived for the promised amniocentesis and ultrasound. As directed, I drank a lot of water before getting on the table. Tom and I had never experienced a prenatal ultrasound. The doctor slathered gel on my abdomen, then moved the mouse around until he could see the baby on the screen. I turned my head to look and was amazed. There was my baby!

Our baby moved around, kicking its legs and looking quite perfect. Now I may not be a doctor or a radiologist. I may not know how to read ultrasounds or x-rays. But this little one sure looked flawless to me. *Lord,* I prayed, *is this baby alright?*

From somewhere in my Spirit came that still small voice I now knew so well. *She is perfect.*

Good enough for me! I sat up. "Never mind," I said to the doctor. "I won't be putting this child at risk by having a test I don't need." I slid down from the exam table, marched to the nearest restroom to empty my bladder, got dressed, and accompanied Tom home.

I had broken a promise. Tom left for his swing shift, angry. The grandparents weren't pleased with me either. My obstetrician phoned me to say he couldn't believe I left without having the test.

Sorry, everyone, but God told me she was perfect.

I sat alone on the living room floor, feeling pretty deflated after my grandstanding gesture in the hospital that afternoon. Mary had been picked up from kindergarten by her grandparents and was spending the night with them.

The phone rang, and I picked myself up and padded into my yellow kitchen. When I heard Allysia's voice at the other end, I thought, *Oh no. What has Mary done at school now? I can't take anything else today.*

"This might sound weird," Allysia began, "but while I was doing my Bible study, the Lord gave me some verses for you. He wants you to have them tonight, Chris. Just please trust Him, and look up these verses. I'm certain they will hold a special meaning for you tonight."

I retrieved my Confirmation Bible from my bedroom and looked up the Scripture in Isaiah.

> *"Woe to him who strives with him who formed him,*
> *a pot among earthen pots!*
> *Does the clay say to him who forms it, 'What are you making?'*
> *or 'Your work has no handles'?*
> *Woe to him who says to a father, 'What are you begetting?'*
> *or to a woman, 'With what are you in labor?'"*
> *Thus says the LORD,*
> *the Holy One of Israel, and the one who formed him:*

> *"Ask me of things to come;*
> *will you command me concerning my children and the*
> *work of my hands?*
> *I made the earth*
> *and created man on it;*
> *it was my hands that stretched out the heavens,*
> *and I commanded all their host.* (Isaiah 45:9–12)

Tears of joy streamed down my face. I fell on my knees and praised the Lord aloud. "Praise the Lord, oh my soul, and all that is within me. Praise his holy name!"

I called Allysia back. This time, I shared what had happened at my doctor's appointment, so she could fully appreciate the meaning and miracle of God giving her those verses for me to read. "Would you be this child's godmother?" I asked. She agreed

At some point, a happy realization dawned on me. When I heard God's reassuring message, *She is perfect,* I had been so focused on the "perfect" part, I didn't think about the "she" part.

I felt strengthened. I was able to encourage Mary to be unafraid. She in turn was free to plan and dream about the fun times ahead with a new sibling. The two would be six years apart, rather than three like she and Sarah had been. Mary colored pictures for the baby, and we hung some in the baby's room.

We retrieved the cradle, which had been out on loan to Liz and Alicia. Helen did her usual thing, creating more beautiful quilts and pictures. My mom knit booties, sweaters, and hats.

Our circle of friends and family was busting at the seams. My sister, Liz, now had three children—two girls and a boy. Gloria was pregnant again, this time with twins. And Alicia was expecting her second child.

In his kindness, God had reached out to us, assuring us he was with us, and we need not worry. Come what may.

11

A Rose and a Thorn

Restore unto me the joy of thy salvation; and uphold me with thy free spirit.

Psalm 51:12 KJV

As we waited for the baby's arrival, we knew one thing for sure. This time, Tom would be my transport to Long Beach Community Hospital. Even if it happened in the middle of the night.

On August 13, 1981 at 3:41 a.m., following a short labor, Anna Marie came into this world. My labor and delivery nurse shed happy tears right along with Tom and me. Because just as promised, she was in perfect health.

When Anna was brought to me for breastfeeding, I said I would first like to spend some time holding and enjoying her. I laid her on my hospital bed, unwrapped her swaddling cloth, and marveled at her beautiful, perfect body. I laughed and cried, as she kicked her tiny legs and pushed her feet against my hand.

Thank you, Lord, for this precious gift!

Loved ones arrived, everyone joyful and relieved. Allysia held up her new godchild, Anna Marie, in the newborn nursery window for Mary to see. After two days, Tom and I were able to leave the hospital *with our daughter in our arms*. A first. After visiting grandparents, we brought Anna home to the pretty room Grandma Helen had helped me redecorate with tiny green rosebuds. We carried the cradle out to our small den, so Anna could hang out with the family.

Mary was excited to be allowed to carry Anna into her bedroom. She set her gently on the bed and lay down next to her. Quickly though, Mary's expression of awe turned to horror when her baby sister threw up on her comforter. We all laughed.

I felt blessed and grateful. My soul praised God. My body and soul were at rest. And I was reminded of Psalm 30:5, "Weeping may tarry for the night, but joy comes with the morning."

God can heal a broken spirit.

I breastfed Anna, and when she was ready for solid food, I had some new, healthier kitchen tricks thanks to Kim's instruction. Anna loved everything I made, even a strange, new-to-us vegetable called rutabaga. As it turned out, we were setting Anna up for a lifetime of healthy and adventurous eating. She would later put the rest of us to shame.

As time went by, Mary and Anna became very close. Anna idolized her big sister, and was so excited each day when Mary came home from school. When Mary donned her Brownie uniform on Girl Scout day, Anna loved to try on her hat.

Just as I had made lifelong friends as a child at Bethany Lutheran, so did Mary. Her two bosom buddies were Leslie and Jennifer.

Leslie was quite shy, and she cried a lot. One day, our phone rang. Leslie's mom, Nancy, was calling just to thank me for

Mary. She told me the story of how Mary had approached Leslie, put her arm around her, and sweetly said, "I will be your friend, *Lesa-lee*."

Years later, Mary and Leslie confessed that when Leslie spent the night, they often took Anna out of her crib to play with her. Good grief, what an undertaking for two tiny girls! Thankfully, Anna survived and was never dropped—at least, to my knowledge.

Weeks turned into years. Little Anna turned three. One day, Mary, Leslie, Jennifer, and Cousin Tina were all over, squeezing out the last drops of summer before fourth grade began. They rode bikes, roller-skated, played in the playhouse, and splashed in our little blow-up pool. All day, they giggled and laughed together. After a dinner barbecue, Tina stayed for a sleepover. The girls bathed and headed to bed.

While Tom and I were still up watching *Saturday Night Live*—this was back in the funny days of Jim Belushi, Billy Crystal, Gilda Radner, and Martin Short—a blood-curdling scream rang out from Mary's room. Rushing in, we found Mary with her head arched back, her waist-long hair dripping with perspiration, and her eyes wide with fright. I called 9-1-1. The paramedics assessed her and then shocked me, saying that because her vital signs were stable, they couldn't transport her to the hospital.

Really? My parents came and picked up Anna and Tina. And while Tom drove us to Miller Children's Hospital in our station wagon, Mary and I rode in the backseat. She rested her head in my lap. I was terrified.

An emergency physician examined Mary. "Has she ridden a bike today?" she asked. We said yes.

"I think she is having a spasm in her buttocks. Take her home, and purchase a better seat for her bike."

My mother bear went into overdrive. *She didn't really just say that to us!* Discernment screamed inside my head and found a voice. "My daughter needs a complete work-up," I insisted. "I know my rights. She is not a hypochondriac, and we are not leaving. You must admit her."

I urged them to call Mary's pediatrician. She had recently been seen by Dr. Krueger for intermittent headaches. He had referred us to a pediatric neurologist, whose first opening for a new patient was still three months away. "I do not want you to touch her or order anything other than a neurological work-up. The way you see her now is not normal for her. Look! She is in horrible pain!"

No way was this the result of a bad bicycle seat. I assured the doctor that something more was going on, and we would get to the bottom of it with or without her help.

Mary was admitted to the medical floor at Miller, where all kinds of specialists began running tests. For five days, she screamed in pain and only received Tylenol. At one point, she had a pain-induced delusion. "Get Happy off of me, Mom! He's too heavy!" Happy was the name of our German shepherd. Mary even chewed the foot off her favorite unicorn stuffed toy. But she had many caring visitors, including her best friend, Leslie, who gave her a small stuffed monkey.

I never left the hospital. Grandparents, extended family, and friends alternated caring for Anna. How we missed our sweet little Anna. But we were heartsick and frightened about what was going on with Mary's health. When my friend Joan, who had been Sarah's preschool teacher, came to check on us, she found me operating on fumes, not eating or showering. Joan was a woman of substance, who I loved and respected. She brought clean clothes and quite literally dragged me into the hospital showers.

Finally, the same neurosurgeon who had operated on Sarah administered a myelogram test, in which they injected dye into Mary's spine. As I was sitting alone in a room just off the testing room, waiting for results, my dear old friend Ladonna suddenly appeared, offering to sit with me. A NICU nurse who had at one time cared for Sarah, Ladonna and I had first met at Bethany Lutheran when her father, Pastor Rutledge, became the assistant pastor. We had also been partners in a self-defense class at Long Beach City College. We must have been a hilarious sight back then—me, standing five-foot-nine-inches, and Ladonna at about five-foot-two.

First Joan. Now Ladonna. God sure seemed to always send just the right people at just the right times. What a wonderful, attentive God, knowing just what we need when we need it.

Tick tock. How slowly time moved as we waited for a verdict. And then, *bingo.* They had finally found the source of Mary's awful pain.

I fully trusted this doctor, who had been through so much with us during Sarah's life. "We have found the problem, Chris," he said. "Mary has a very large, hemorrhaging mass running the length of her spine. Her nervous system went into shock when the mass grew too large for her spinal column. Saturday night, it burst." He went on to apologize for allowing her to endure such excruciating pain and to inform us she was being transferred to the ICU, where she would receive heavy medication for her pain.

"She must have surgery tomorrow," he continued. "You'll need to come with me to sign the surgical consent." I followed, trying to take it all in, feeling a deep sense of fondness and appreciation for his sincerity and empathy. But his next words were sobering. "I can't believe I am standing here, having to tell you that I do not know if I can save Mary's life. I do not know what the hemorrhaging tissue is, but I have to try to cauterize the bleeding and remove the tissue. If I can't get the tissue out and it continues to hemorrhage, Mary will die. I am so sorry, Chris."

I was in a daze, hanging on to what I knew. I could trust him to do his very best. And the rest was up to God.

The family waiting room was jam-packed with concerned family and friends praying together and trying to bring Tom and I some comfort. I felt like I was smothering. I had to go have a come-to-Jesus meeting. Now.

Here I was again, back in the same chapel I knew too well. The place I had come so often, a desperate mother, kneeling and pleading for God's mercy. A righteous rage exploded in me. I balled up my fists and began screaming at God. I even flipped him off.

"Why, why, why have you forsaken me?" I screamed, borrowing from Psalm 22. "Is it not enough you took Sarah from me? I cannot lose Mary too! People claim you never give us more than we can handle. Well, I'm putting you on notice that I can't handle losing Mary. Enough, Lord! Have mercy on Mary and me!"

The surgery took forever long. At last, the doctor entered the family room. He was visibly exhausted and asked if he could have a chair to sit down. I held my breath. Finally, he smiled. "Her toes are wiggling. I was able to remove all of the tissue."

I leaped up, hugged the doctor, and thanked him. Then I excused myself and ran back to the chapel. On my knees, I burst into grateful tears. "Thank you, Lord Jesus!" And I knew. It was okay to have felt angry, like I couldn't go on.

God never minds when we cry out to him, as the psalmists did. When we do, we find him, the one who, in the person of Jesus, suffers right along with us.

God was faithful to meet me in this unforeseen mess, in my weakness, in my pain. Just as he promised.

> *But he said to me, "My grace is sufficient for you, for my power is made perfect in weakness." Therefore, I will boast all the more gladly of my weaknesses, so that the power of Christ may rest upon me. For the sake of Christ, then, I am content with weaknesses, insults, hardships, persecutions, and calamities. For when I am weak, then I am strong.*
>
> 2 Corinthians 12:9–10

12

A Word and a Way

I can do all things through him who strengthens me.

Philippians 4:13

My friend Judy is also a woman of substance. Another strong woman with a giant heart. And she was the perfect, God-sent person to speak a hard word of truth to me.

A couple days after Mary's surgery, Judy and I sat together on my cot in Mary's hospital room. Judy was an RN, and her son Mikey had been in Sarah's preschool class. As Mary lay in her bed playing with paper dolls, a woman bounced through the door. She wore a pinafore-style apron and carried a basket with a bow on the handle.

She was extremely friendly and pleasant. "Is this Mary's room?" she asked. "Are you her mother?"

I nodded absently.

"May I sit down?"

As she spoke, she pulled some pamphlets out of her basket and handed them to me. "I want to welcome you and Mary to our cancer club. I have parking passes here for you since you'll be coming to the hospital regularly for Mary's treatments. We also have a support group for siblings of children with cancer. Sometimes, you see, they get overlooked. Left behind. We also have support groups for parents and . . ."

I'd heard enough. "I'm sorry, but you have the wrong room. Wrong patient. Mary does not have cancer." Stunned and horrified, I tried to collect myself. "And what parent in their right mind would want to be welcomed to a cancer club as if it was a lifetime pass to Disneyland, anyway?"

Before I could totally explode, Judy jumped up, snagging the decorated basket with one hand and the pinafore-lady's arm with the other. She tossed the basket into the hallway, guided the woman out of the room, and shut the door. She then led me into the bathroom and locked the door behind us.

Judy put her hands on my shoulders. "Chris, look at me. Mary does have cancer."

I collapsed onto the antiseptic-smelling floor. "No! No, no, no," I sobbed. Judy just held me tight while I wailed.

Oh, what a lesson in the power of words. During all of Mary's tests and her surgery, the words I'd heard used were *tissue*, *hemorrhage*, and *cluster*. No one ever spoke *cancer* or *tumor*.

I had been under the impression that a successful surgery meant Mary was out of the woods. Perhaps I'd been floating gently down that old river called *de-nial* until I was better able to absorb the real truth of our situation. The only other harsh reality I'd accepted was that Mary's beautiful, long hair, which had been mangled into a huge, impossible knot, had needed to be chopped short. She looked cute. But now my mind reeled with questions. Among them, would she require chemotherapy and lose her hair altogether?

Thank God, he had sent Judy when I needed someone strong to lean on. Unbeknownst to us, a few years later, God would divinely orchestrate an opportunity for me to return the favor. When her son, Mikey, passed away, Judy asked me to speak at his memorial service. What a humbling honor to publicly proclaim Judy's loving ways and her devotion to her son.

I learned another thing through the basket-lady incident and the events that followed: Health professionals must always, always be certain, before meeting with a patient and their family, that the doctor in charge of the case has already given the patient and family a clear diagnosis. Because not long after the basket lady was tossed out of the room, Mary's two assigned oncologists paid us a visit.

Now, at last, I learned Mary's diagnosis. She had an *ependymoma*, a brain tumor lodged in the *neural tube*, or spinal column.

One of the two physicians recommended chemotherapy. The other, radiation.

"Why are you in disagreement about the course of treatment?" I asked.

Following an intense discussion beyond Mary's earshot, I was forced to kick them off her case. Although they were renowned pediatric oncologists and I had great respect for them, they readily admitted they had no experience with Mary's type of cancer. So they were only guessing at the best course of treatment, hoping to cover all the bases.

I recognized this was one of those key times I needed to rely on my discernment and advocate for my child. And my child needed a referral to a specialist.

We received one.

Two weeks later, Tom, Mary, and I flew north to consult a wonderful pediatric oncologist and neurosurgeon at the University of California at San Francisco (UCSF). He determined a clear regimen of therapy. Mary would receive the maximum amount of radiation, five thousand *rads*. Chemotherapy, we learned, would not work on an ependymoma cell. Our UCSF specialist coordinated with Miller Children's Hospital for local radiation treatments and five years of spinal taps. This way, we wouldn't have to move to San Francisco or travel constantly.

There was some deliberation about doing surgery to move Mary's ovaries out of the way of radiation. *Good grief, she isn't even close to puberty*, I worried. Who knew what the long-term outcome of this kind of surgery on a nine-year-old might be. In the end, shielding blocks were used prevent radiation from affecting her ovaries.

I kept all these things tucked away in my heart.

They warn that even good marriages can fall prey to prolonged seasons of stress. And ours had certainly undergone more than its share. Following Mary's cancer catastrophe, Tom and I began truly unraveling. We fought regularly. The tension in our home was palpable.

Tom was fried. He had been working hard for so long, even on the weekends, to make ends meet. But when he asked me to get a job outside the house, I flipped out. I had long desired to pursue my master's degree in social work, but for years Tom had heartily disapproved. He pointed out that I had a college degree that I had never used. "Why do you need another degree to stay home, have babies, and make cookies?" he would say.

Still, even with my dream denied, I wanted to contribute to the family finances. But how could I take a job that required leaving sweet Anna, who was still a toddler, and Mary, who had just undergone cancer surgery and was in treatments?

One day, our Lutheran insurance agent, Bob, stopped by to deliver a policy and found me sitting at our kitchen table, crying. I explained my predicament; I didn't want to leave my daughters and work outside the home. Bob suggested I sell insurance. I could have a home office, he said, and I'd only occasionally need to leave the girls for evening appointments. *Me, sell insurance?* Okay, I would give it a try!

I passed all the necessary tests and, for the next four years, worked as an AAL (Aid Association for Lutherans), selling life insurance. I wasn't super successful, but I did qualify for their lower-level conferences.

The day came when I had to tell Helen a divorce was imminent. "Oh, I know, honey. I know," she said in her Oklahoma drawl. "I'm sorry. I wish things were different."

"It doesn't interfere with my love for you," I said.

"Nor mine for you."

In 1987, we both remarried—two weeks apart. Tom married Rosie, who shared his love of horses, and I married Bob, the insurance salesman. Both of us were much happier. Still, I shed many a tear, feeling like I had failed at keeping the family together. One day, Mary said something that stunned me. "Stop crying, Mom. I'm glad you and Dad are not fighting anymore. I like Rosie, and I like Bob. We will all be better off."

After enduring five years of spinal taps to screen for cancer cells, Mary was considered cured. Praise the Lord! Now attending the same high school where her dad and I had met, Mary tried out for the drill team and made it.

In 1989, I dared again to resurrect my dream. I carried ten large manila envelopes out to the garage, where Bob was working. "These ten envelopes from CSULB carry postmarks from each of the last ten years. They're the applications for their graduate MSW program that I have had to set aside. Bob, I believe this is what God wants me to do. Are you okay with me applying for the program?"

He gave me his blessing. Soon I was on track to graduate in 1991.

Meanwhile, it seemed nothing about Mary's life was going to come easy. In her sophomore year, she could no longer sit at her desk in school without horrible pain. She tried bringing a pillow to school for her back, but that didn't help. So it was back to a neurosurgeon, who reported that Mary's backbones were crumbling to dust. The radiation had done its job well, killing the cancer cells. But it had also destroyed her spine.

Mary would have to undergo a massive surgery—spinal fusion. Her godparents, Jill and Glenn, drove up from San Diego to be present. The poignant way Glenn looked at Mary when she was wheeled back to her room after surgery would forever be etched on my heart. Tears rolled down his cheeks. He had to turn his head away.

We all knew Mary had another long road ahead of her.

Sure enough, many, many physical and occupational therapies were required for her to relearn the basics. Just putting on her socks and shoes was a huge undertaking. Let alone, walking. Cocooned inside a body cast for several months, followed by a back brace, she had no choice but to drop drill team. She learned to drive while wearing her "turtle shell."

Adolescence would have been tough enough without all Mary had to deal with on top of it.

About a year after this process, Mary had to face yet another surgery, to remove all the hardware used to put her spine back together. By now, I'd begun work as a full-time medical social worker. So when Mary was finally discharged from the hospital, Grandma Helen and Grandpa Paul picked her up and brought her to their house. They also drove to the elementary school to scoop up Anna, who was by now a busy and beautiful nine-year-old.

13

A Purpose Revealed

⟶

And we know that for those who love God all things work together for good, for those who are called according to his purpose.

Romans 8:28

While I was raising kids for fifteen years, technology was leaving me behind. I still didn't even know how to type. Now here I was, back in the classroom at CSULB, completely intimidated.

Miraculously, I had passed the GRE and been admitted into the Master of Social Work program. I reminded myself that, although I lacked classroom experience, I sure had wheelbarrows-full of life experience.

During one of my first classes, I was seated next to a red-headed man who looked like he could be a football player. His feet were propped up on the desk in front of him, and his tennis shoes were untied. Our professor handed each of us a sheet of paper with a case vignette typed out. Our assignment was to write out our assessment and diagnosis based on the *Diagnostic and Statistical Manual of Mental Disorders* (DSM) handbook.

I raised my hand. "I'm sorry, but I think I must be in the wrong class. I have no idea what you are asking on this piece of paper."

Her voice was kind and reassuring. "Sounds like you are in exactly the right class."

I looked around me. Everyone, including the brawny redhead, was busy writing their answers. I stared at my blank page feeling like a total failure. This would be impossible.

The redhead, who introduced himself as Thomas, said something to make me laugh. It was all I needed to survive that moment. And moment by moment, I made it through the program, armed with faith . . . and a sense of humor.

Little by little, the trunk of my car filled up with brown grocery bags. Each bag was marked with a number, indicating which chapter of my work-in-progress graduate thesis it held. All of it was handwritten on yellow legal pads. Most days, I would deliver Anna and Mary to their respective activities—gymnastics, piano lessons, softball games, swim meets—then pop open my trunk, grab a bag of notes and research, and work on it while watching the girls.

When I finally completed my thesis, I had to pay a professional typist five hundred dollars to type it in the correct format.

Funny as it sounds, my thesis was entitled "Depression among Lutheran Women of the Sandwich Generation." I guess I'm nothing if not consistent—and Lutheran. The Lutheran Church, with Jesus as cornerstone, was the rock on which I was founded, and it had stood strong though life's storms and quakes.

We often refer only to pastors, parochial schoolteachers, missionaries, theologians, and the like as having been "called by God" into their roles. I have to disagree. Others can be equally called to their professions. I knew beyond a shadow of a doubt that my Lord and Savior had been calling me to serve his people in a social worker capacity. As sure as the ocean's tide, life can pull you toward your life's work, as if by divine design.

To my mind, I had been in social work ever since 1978, when Sarah was born.

Ready or not, I had then been inducted into the world of children with special needs and of parents with courage and stamina. I met women with incredible insight and wit. I observed how often, when a child is born with special needs, the mother stands strong but the father leaves. Sadly, this was the case with a majority of the families I encountered on my journey with Sarah.

During Sarah's lifetime, most of my days and nights were spent at Miller Children's Hospital, either at the outpatient therapy center, the inpatient floor of the hospital, or the lab. I was a regular at Tichenor Orthopedic Clinic and preschool as well. And Mary had her own appointments. I ushered her to the Scottish Rite for speech therapy and to a tutoring center when she needed help in the second grade.

Sarah's world became Mary's world as well as mine. Some people are uncomfortable being around doctors and hospitals. But Mary and I became very used to a medical setting.

After Sarah died, her teacher, Joan, asked me to come back to the Tichenor preschool and start a parent support group. Initially I said, "No way." I was still too raw with grief, wrestling with inner demons, wallowing in shame and self-pity. After losing a child, one can't help expecting that, out of respect, the world should come to a halt. At least for a time. But it doesn't.

Alas, grief is a very personal experience, and there's no magic formula or timeframe for moving through the process.

But Joan kept insisting I "get back in the saddle." I thought and prayed about it. Finally, I realized I had not only devoured all those books about parenting a disabled child and about losing a child to death, I had also lived these experiences and, sort of, survived. I told Joan I would try my best.

As it turned out, meeting weekly with other mothers and their children was balm for my shattered heart, helping me to heal as well as them. Witnessing their compassion toward one another was humbling. The raw and real humor we exchanged uplifted us all. No topics were too sensitive. These were combat moms. Each had experienced their own kind of battles.

We began fellowshipping outside the preschool as well and chose to call our group F.A.C.E. FORWARD (Family and Community Effort). Our purpose was to foster a forward-facing posture. To encourage each other and our communities to look to what was ahead in real time, not succumbing to a stagnant, what-should-have-been mentality. Together, we could learn to accept our new normal and move forward.

We designed brochures, held meetings, threw each other baby showers. We attended kids' birthday parties and, sometimes, funerals. We were comrades in the trenches, together navigating the world of special-needs children, broken promises, broken marriages, and shattered dreams.

Although I later learned vital academic theories in graduate school, my personal experiences and the families I met threw Tichenor and Miller Children's Hospital would always prove to be my best teachers.

After graduating with my MSW in August of 1991, my first job was at a locked *geropsychiatric* facility, working with older adults at a time when Alzheimer's was just becoming recognized and long-term care facilities were popping up all over the country.

I got my feet wet in the world of social work alongside renowned psychiatrists Dr. Stephen Reed, Dr. Abes Bagheri, and Dr. Branko Radisavljevic. At the Douglas French Center, of which Dr. Reed was program director, I gained firsthand experience with psychiatric problems and treatments. I learned how to write *t-cons* (temporary conservatorships). And how not to get punched.

It only happened to me once in all my years of social work. As I was rounding up the patients for our morning group, one woman stayed behind with her head down on the dining room table, crying. Gently I rubbed her back and asked what was wrong. She motioned me to come closer, so she could whisper to me. Naively, I did, and she popped me right in the face with her closed fist.

So, I take it you prefer not to join us for group this morning.

Other than my pride, I wasn't seriously injured. *But girl,* I thought, *you still have a lot to learn.*

In 1994, while working in geropsychiatry, I received *the* call. This was exactly the work God had long been preparing me for. I was stunned. I was honored. I was thrilled!

Darlene, administrator of the Geraldine A. Stramski Children's Chronic Disease Center at Miller Children's Hospital, contacted me to ask if I might be interested in applying for their social worker position. Their person was about to retire.

I couldn't believe my ears. This was the clinic where I'd taken Sarah for her developmental checkups and therapy. Yes, indeed I was interested! I was born for this. In fact, my first assignment was to launch a support group for parents and preteen adolescents with spina bifida.

And they said you didn't have a plan, Lord!

After all was said and done, I had "come home" to serve the families, patients, and staff of Long Beach Memorial, where I and my daughters had been born, and Miller Children's Hospital, where Mary and Sarah had received intense medical care from 1978 through 1985. Now, the year was 1994. How patient we sometimes have to be, before we see God's plans come to fruition.

Dr. Stramski, who founded the center, had passed away, but I remembered her gentle, caring guidance to Sarah and me as we wrestled with understanding Sarah's development. I was over the moon with the opportunity and honored Darlene put her trust in me. As if that wasn't enough, God placed a cherry on top when Darlene introduced me to the woman who would be my partner in the parent support group. There, sitting in a chair in Darlene's office and wearing a green sweater was the prettiest woman, with the brightest, most beautiful smile I had ever seen.

Judy Walker had a sparkle in her eyes and one of the most joyous spirits I ever had the pleasure of knowing. Not only was Judy beautiful, funny, and dedicated, she was also brilliant. We quickly became the best of friends. With her master's degree in nursing, Judy was a clinical nurse specialist. We took to working together like two ducks in water. And our spina bifida group succeeded wildly.

While I met with the parents in a conference room at the back of the clinic, Judy met with the kids, all of whom were entering puberty, with all the social pressures and adjustments that encompasses. She had a way of discussing the most sensitive subjects with the patients. They shared about self-catheterizing and school dances. Judy empowered them, and more than once had them laughing so hard someone would throw up.

I had many fruitful discussions with the parents' support group as well, discussing hard issues out of earshot of their pre-teens. We held Christmas parties for the families. Judy and I wrapped all the gifts, which had been donated by community partners, and one of the dads always dressed up as Santa.

Not all was fun and games. Once, a mother and her son came into the clinic for an appointment. Because he was unable to walk, he needed special shoes and treatment for foot sores. A week later, we received the tragic news that their home had become engulfed in flames. The mom covered her son with her own body, and they both died. I so admired this act of mother-bear dedication, protecting her son, who couldn't save himself.

Judy and I were also on the cranial facial team at the hospital, working with patients born with cleft palates. We helped the stunned parents of newborns with this defect figure out how to feed them. And working as part of an interdisciplinary team, we supported oral surgeons, orthodontists, ear, nose, and throat doctors, speech therapists, and plastic surgeons who treated these patients' needs through age eighteen. Meeting monthly for dinner, our dedicated team discussed each case, collaborating on treatment plans. Following these kids as they matured was nothing short of amazing.

Judy and I also worked with children diagnosed with LP (little person), autism spectrum disorder, attention deficit and attention deficit hyperactive disorders, and Down syndrome. I cherished my meaningful work at the Stramski Developmental

Clinic and was honored to labor alongside Judy in this capacity. We were making a lifetime of poignant memories.

Change Is God

One day Mary called me from Chico with an announcement that left me speechless. "Hi, Mom," she said. "I have news. I've changed my major to social work. Mom . . . Mom . . . are you still there?"

I was so stunned I had to hang up and call her back. Mary, who in many ways was her father's daughter and didn't like to talk about feelings, wanted to go into social work? How had it happened? How could she switch horses in the middle of the race, losing college credits, starting over? What about her life-long dream to be a teacher?

When I called her back, she was laughing about the fact that, for the first time in her life, she had me at a loss of words. Her counselor had helped her figure everything out, and she could still graduate on schedule.

Well, shut my mouth! What do you know? "Honey," I said, "you do know social workers have to talk with people about emotions."

In 1996, I received my Licensed Clinical Social Worker (LCSW), which requires a master's degree in social work, successful completion of two years of supervised, full-time work in the field, and a passing grade on the state exam. This was, for me, a grueling process. I dreaded the computerized test more than the oral exam. When I passed both, I cried so dramatically, Bob thought I had failed.

The first thing I did when I received my license in the mail was call my dad.

"That's great, Honey! Now go and do God's work. Oh, and when you have a chance, I could use a haircut."

That very afternoon, my dad suffered a massive cerebral hemorrhage. Afterward, he could only speak with great difficulty. When Anna and I visited him in the emergency room, her beautiful blue eyes spilled over with tears. Grandpa lifted his one working arm, took her hand, and asked, "How was your swim meet today, honey?"

"It was good, Grandpa. We won."

In addition to her performing talents, Anna had found her niche on the high school swimming and water polo teams, taking to the water like a fish. All the family enjoyed watching her literally plow through the water in competitions.

Seventeen days after Dad's stroke, I attended another of Anna's swim meets, secretly carrying the news that my dad had died that morning. I would wait and tell her after the competition. Sitting alone in the stands at the Belmont Plaza swimming pool, I cheered for Anna's last relay.

"Go, honey, go!" I shouted. "Swim for Grandpa!" Anna won. Afterward, I took her outside, onto the beach, where we walked barefoot on the sand. I handed her a congratulatory bouquet of flowers. "Grandpa watched you win that relay from heaven, honey," I said. We held each other and cried.

Less than two weeks before his stroke, Dad had sung before the Bethany Lutheran congregation on Easter Sunday. After he passed, I received a poignant note from Carol, the choir director, exclaiming with wonder how fitting it was that Dad had graduated to a heavenly choir on the heels of singing about the eternal hope we have because of Jesus' resurrection.

When I contracted a bad upper respiratory infection following Dad's death, I was hospitalized for a week and given breathing treatments. Mary wisely said to me, "You know, Mom, our grief is stored in our lungs."

Hmm. So there it was. I had enough grief to fill up both lungs.

With Dad gone, Mom became even feistier and required more of my attention. Meanwhile, I was struggling personally at the clinic, as changing winds complicated my work. Truth be told, I was still a mom who had survived my child's death. I had always been overly sensitive. As much as I hated leaving Judy, I caved under the pressure of it all and quit in 1997.

I thought perhaps I could help out Bob in his insurance office. But much to my surprise, he didn't think that was the best idea.

Okay. *Now what, Lord?* I took a position at another locked geropsychiatric unit, Passages, which was a part of St. Mary's Hospital. Here I had the pleasure of reconnecting with Dr. Branko. I led some inpatient groups and also worked with the elderly who came into the outpatient clinic. Expanding on my social-work skills, I became licensed as a psychiatric evaluation team (PET) member. On occasion, I would go into the bowels of Long Beach and Los Angeles County to assess geriatric folks who might be homicidal, suicidal, or gravely disabled.

One hot summer afternoon, I went out on a call to assess an elderly woman who was living under the stairs of an apartment complex. She had water, newspapers to sleep on, and shelter from the heat. But she was a shade of orange I'd only ever seen in someone in the final stages of liver failure. Even the whites of her eyes were dark orange. The woman strongly disagreed with my decision that she be transported by ambulance to St. Mary's for evaluation.

"I understand, ma'am," I said. "But I have to write a 5150 for you, calling for a seventy-two-hour hold, because I believe you are gravely ill and need medical attention."

When later I entered the emergency room to check on my patient's status, I was shocked to learn that her labs had checked out okay. I questioned the doctor who said he was releasing her back to her world under the stairs. "What? I don't understand. Then why is she that color?"

It turned out the woman was a vegetarian who ate mostly carrots. Another lesson learned—gratitude for those systems of checks and balances that keep us humble and grounded. For weeks I was subjected to Bugs Bunny jokes and carrots left on my desk.

As much as I enjoyed working with Dr. Branko, I missed my "home" at Memorial. So I reached out to the social work director, Donna, to inquire about what jobs were available. Donna explained that my position at the Stramski Clinic was filled when I left. So instead I was hired to work in the clinic where doctors in residency practice. This came as we were emerging from the dark ages, before computerized patient charts, when all documentation was done in writing. It was how I had learned, and frankly, it was just my speed. But time and technology marched on. Ugh. I either had to get on board or be left behind.

I enjoyed working with the residents, who were completing their doctor training before moving on to their specialties and practices. I also worked with expectant women with high-risk pregnancies due to domestic violence, poor nutrition, gestational diabetes, poverty, or all of the above. This was an eye-opener. One such mom asked if I would stand by in the delivery room when she gave birth to her son, who was expected to have multiple birth anomalies and defects. I assured her that, of course, I would be present.

While the woman was understandably anxious, she approached her due date bravely. She wanted this baby. I could relate. I worked closely with a wonderful Christian chaplain named Sharon, who was tender, prayerful, and experienced in ministering to high-risk mothers. While Sharon waited outside the delivery room, I held the mom's hand throughout her c-section.

The baby boy had all his parts. He cried at birth just like a newborn should. And he was adorable. Her son had some complications, but he lived. When the mother came to the clinic for her six-week checkup, she showed off her baby to our team with pride and joy. We all marveled together.

Donna found the light in me I did not know I had. She asked me to supervise the LCSW candidates who were working toward their licensure. What an honor to teach the ladies . . . and learn from them too.

Donna presented me with yet another opportunity. And when she introduced me to Pastor Feleti, the same kind of divine alignment seemed to take place as when I was introduced to Judy Walker. Feleti was an ordained Presbyterian minister from Samoa, a former diplomat for the Polynesian islands. The pastor and I were to become the inpatient palliative care team, working closely with the seventh-floor ICU and occasionally the emergency department, in support of families dealing with worst-case-scenario news about their loved ones—terminal diagnoses or brain death. I was again on a blessed, God-orchestrated journey with the perfect partner. Feleti and I were like soup and sandwich. Salt and pepper. You get the idea.

Feleti and I began each day in Memorial Chapel, the very same chapel where I had spent my most desperate moments praying over Sarah and Mary and crying out to God. Think of it! *What a sweet God you are, redeeming my pain in this way, Father!*

From day to day, we never knew exactly what we might be asked to face, only that the situation would be tragic and without cure. Together we prayed for the right words to give patients and family members. Our faith guided and sustained us as we comforted people of all cultures, faiths, and customs. In awe, we watched God work.

One woman who was dying of cancer had taken great pains to write out a few important questions for her oncologist. Alert, but unable to speak due to a ventilator tube down her throat, she asked me to help present these questions to her doctor. I will never forget the pain in her eyes when the doctor wadded up the paper she had laboriously written. "I do not know if or when you will die," he said flippantly. "I could be killed walking across the street today. I'm not God."

After he left the room, she looked at me with tears streaming. Her eyes begged for answers and help. "I have this," I said. "No worries. You'll get your answers if I have to tackle him." I yelled the physician's name down the hallway. "Stop!"

He turned around. "What do you want from me?"

"The truth, doctor. Give her the truth!"

He returned to her room, picked up the wadded paper and smoothed it out. Reading each question, he answered as honestly as he could. The woman squeezed his hand and mouthed the words the words "Thank you." Her eyes now held peace. Now she knew what she needed to do.

We helped facilitate understanding in her husband, who wasn't accepting her terminal diagnosis. Then we helped bring this patient's last wish to pass. She had wanted to go to the islands but was too ill to travel. Feleti had a marvelous idea: he would bring the islands to her. The whole floor participated. We decorated her room with posters of the islands and other tropical décor. Feleti's nieces performed a Polynesian dance, in full costume and draped with real Hawaiian leis. And then my jaw about hit the floor when Feleti bounded into the patient's room and executed a traditional warrior dance—shirtless. Joy abounded, and our dying friend clapped her hands in glee.

In another case, a doctor entered a woman's hospital room and spoke into her ear the bleak outcome of her scans and tests. She would never be cured. Like the other cancer patient, she couldn't speak through a breathing tube. When she received the doctor's news, she just pointed toward the big windows and smiled. We knew she was pointing to heaven. Her entire family gathered around her bed as her ventilator was turned off.

One by one, the patient's husband and adult children said goodbye. Her son held a photo of his newborn twins before her. This faith-filled woman knew exactly where she was going, and she was ready. What an honor and privilege to stand with her family members, praying and singing her through heaven's pearly gates. She died wearing a peaceful smile.

I've often asked myself, How many of us have that kind of faith? And what are we willing to suffer through in order to obtain it?

I will forever be grateful to Donna for her friendship, her leadership, and her belief in my abilities. A few years later, in the summer of 2004, I would have the honor of reading the Bible passage at her lovely wedding to Kit.

Few things in my life have been more fulfilling or faith-affirming than my work with Feleti, helping people pass into their eternal place of rest. I was given the nickname AOD, for Angel of Death, a title that humbled me.

14

A Future and a Hope

For I know the plans I have for you, declares the Lord, *plans for welfare and not for evil, to give you a future and a hope.*

Jeremiah 29:11

Mary loved taking photos, so when Anna wanted to practice for getting her professional head shots taken, we all headed to Seal Beach and made a fun day of it. Mary set the scene while I lugged all the clothing changes.

With Anna, the first child I was allowed to carry home from the hospital, we enjoyed many more firsts. First boyfriend, a varsity water polo player. First prom. Judy Walker came over and we took lots of pictures. Until now, I had been denied these typical high school activities that many families take for granted. I'd had no opportunity to participate as a parent in extracurricular activities with Mary except for one season of drill team, before her back crumbled.

Once, Anna traveled with her youth group to North Carolina to dig trenches and build houses for homeless folks. And always, she pursued acting. After performing in the comedy "Pillow Talk" and "The Sound of Music," she blew us away in her first leading role, as Stella in the "A Street Car Named Desire." Following one of her high school plays, one of her youth leaders commented, "Anna reminds me of a combination of Grace Kelly and Meryl Streep on stage." I agreed with her and added, "You really must throw in some Carol Burnett too!"

In high school, Anna met her other lifetime best friend, Jaclyn. These two tall, beautiful young women had a zest for life and jumped at the chance to participate in a school trip to Italy. I always told my daughters I would never clip their wings just to control them. I promised to be supportive and let them fly. Sometimes this cost me dearly.

Mary went on to get her master's degree in social work from my old alma mater, CSULB. I was so overcome with pride; I took the opportunity to finally throw her a huge party to celebrate her accomplishments and triumphs. Although still shy, she was a great sport.

We decorated with her favorite color, purple, prepared a feast of her favorite foods, and hired a DJ. The dancing began with her favorite song, "Brown-Eyed Girl." I lined up people from every stage of Mary's life to participate in a game of "Mary, This Is Your Life!" One at a time, each person hid behind a curtain, while Mary asked questions to solve their identity. Mary guessed everyone correctly—even Barry Ceverha, the doctor who had operated on her cancer and performed the five years of spinal taps.

"Mary," he said, giving her a clue, "I am probably the only man who has ever seen your backside naked beside your dad."

Around one hundred friends and family helped commemorate Mary's fortitude and achievements. When Leslie and Anna read tributes they had composed, I cried tears of joy. Later, Mary said to me, "It was like a wedding reception without a groom!"

After graduating with her MSW, Mary went to work as a social worker in pediatric rehabilitation at a children's hospital. But not just any children's hospital. Here was another major God-wink.

She now worked at Miller, the very hospital that provided the backdrop for so much of her life story. You can't make this stuff up!

While I was still working on the same campus, at Long Beach Memorial, I liked to go down to the basement gym where Mary worked with the children, and marvel. Here, in this very same gym, Mary's baby sister Sarah used to work out every week with her beloved physical therapist, Sandy. I could easily close my eyes and envision Mary age at age four, jumping around the pediatric gym, making Sarah laugh. Now my eyes were opened, to wonder at the woman Mary had become and at how God had redeemed the painful road that brought her here.

Meanwhile, I wasn't surprised when adventurous Anna opted to do college far away. Majoring in film and television, she began her higher education in Boston, where she was given the opportunity to design her own internship. Anna would be interning with legendary actor Jon Voight! Lucky for me, that meant she would have to return for a while to Los Angeles.

On that fateful morning of September 11, 2001, Bob and I sat glued to the television along with everyone else in America. Anna was showering, getting ready to head to her internship in LA. She came out of the bathroom with a towel wrapped around her head and saw our tense faces. "What's going on?"

Together we all watched in horror as the planes crashed and buildings collapsed. Anna and I exchanged a knowing look.

That was the same airline flight out of Boston she took to LA.
Out loud, we praised God she had been home today and not
on that flight.

Anna and her Italian girlfriend, Renee, decided to change
colleges to Hofstra University in New York because her friend's
major was not available in Boston. So only a couple of weeks
after 9/11, I made my first trip to New York City. Such dust
and devastation. The grief and patriotism were palpable. Renee's
family hosted us for a visit in their New Jersey home. Hearing her
father, who sang in an amazing *shoo-boop-de-bop* group, brought
back fun memories of my dad and uncles singing together.

Now majoring in communication, with an emphasis in
media, television, and entertainment, Anna returned to our side
of the country to finish out her bachelor's at Biola University in
southern California. She may have been living in the dorms, but
to me she was home! Her graduation party featured a karaoke
machine in the living room, with Uncle Butch and others singing together, of course. By now, Mary had moved out and was
living by the beach. Bob had moved his successful insurance
business out of our home and into an office in Orange County.
Life was about as good as it could get. Then Anna threw me a
giant curve ball.

She and a friend had decided to move to Boston.

Ugh. And I had promised never to clip her wings. Alas,
it was her choice. Anna found work in Boston and for several
years was happy there.

When Aid Association for Lutherans merged with Lutheran
Brotherhood Insurance Company to become Thrivent, and Bob
didn't agree with some of their policies, he signed on with One
America. Bob continued to thrive and feel fulfilled by his work
with clients. One America even did a feature piece on Bob in

one of their monthly magazines. They quoted him saying, "I will never retire. I love what I do!"

In the summer of 2004, Bob asked if we could please cancel our reservations at a coastal bed and breakfast. Instead he wanted to take a drive up to Bend, Oregon. "Where?" I asked, not doing a very good job of masking my disappointment. "Why?"

"Thirty-seven golf courses," he explained. He'd read that Bend was a great place to retire.

"Are you retiring?"

"No," he said.

"There are lots of golf courses in southern California too," I said. But honestly, Bob rarely asked me for anything. So I agreed.

We drove, we saw, we fell in love with the quaint town of Bend. We bought a beautiful home, leased it out for a year, sold our Long Beach house, and moved north in November of 2005. "Quit your job," Bob said. "You don't have to work anymore."

A month later I found myself on the kitchen floor, sobbing, after receiving that fateful call I shared about in the opening chapter. Our courageous young friend Brianna had been killed in a bus accident while doing mission work in Nigeria. Why, Lord? Her death seemed to have been preventable, thanks to my prophetic dream. When pressed, God said, *Her life and her death were destined to bring me glory.*

Ah. Just like Sarah's life and death. I get it, Lord. I don't have to see it now. You've proven yourself more than faithful to redeem our family's pain.

You never waste a tear.

Besides, as the apostle Paul said, "To live is Christ, and to die is gain" (Philippians 1:21). I still couldn't very well explain such mysteries, but I could look for ways to proclaim the blessedness of living like Brianna. Fearlessly.

After experimenting with retirement for fourteen months, which really didn't really work, I became a primary-care social worker for the Veterans Administration. The good Lord had placed us right where he wanted us and again given me just the right supervisor to guide and support me in a new capacity. Yvette was brilliant, sensitive, and knowledgeable about the veterans' health system. She allowed me to do my job with conviction, knowing beyond a shadow of a doubt she had my back.

I told my coworkers I would be working in service to veterans until the day I died. "If ever I don't answer my phone, you'll have to come pick up my dead head off my keyboard. 'Cuz I'll be singing in the pearly gates of heaven!"

Anna surprised Bob and me with two pieces of news. First, she had decided to go back to school to become a registered nurse, which absolutely floored me. Second, she had ended her current romantic relationship, and she was ready to move on. In fact, she wanted to come live with us in Bend and knock out her prerequisites here. She didn't have to ask us twice!

Anna came, studied, made new friends, and then was accepted to the bachelor's RN programs at both Johns Hopkins University and Indiana University Purdue University Indiana (IUPUI). Anna chose IUPUI, and that is where she met Kevin.

Like Anna, Kevin had already acquired a degree in a different endeavor. He had also served in the Navy for a couple of years, as had his father and brother, Kyle. When Anna drastically altered her spring break plans despite having a roundtrip ticket home to Bend, I knew she had truly fallen in love. In the middle of one night, she phoned, crying, to say that Kyle's wife had just died of breast cancer. She and Kevin would drive to

Ohio to pick up Kyle and bring him home. What tragic news. I encouraged her to drive carefully and then get to the airport for her flight to Bend.

"Mom," she said, "I'm not leaving Kevin and his family at such a devastating time."

Lord, what is happening? Is this the man I've been praying to you about since Anna was born? Is he a godly man who will love and cherish her and be a wonderful, caring father to their children?

In my spirit, I heard the Lord say yes. This was the man. And so it was.

Our Anna made such a beautiful bride. I thanked God for this union, and for friends and family that came from near and far to Indiana in August of 2013 to share in this most joyous occasion. This definitely called for music and family tradition! The night before the wedding, I and my siblings, Juss and Liz, along with our cousin Jill, serenaded Anna and Kevin with the Andrews Sisters' song "Apple Blossom Time," just as my dad and my aunts and uncles had done for weddings past. Having all grown up with the song, we needed no rehearsal. What a poignant moment for all of us.

When Tom walked Anna down the aisle, her eyes were fixed on Kevin, and tears streamed down her cheeks. During the ceremony, cousins Alicia and Valerie, as well as Bob and our good friend Mike, joined our little singing group. It felt as if all our loved ones in heaven sang along through the words of the musical benediction "The Lord Bless You and Keep You."

Shortly after they were married, I traveled to Indianapolis for a visit. Anna had purchased tickets for the three of us to go downtown and see a play, "The Diary of Anne Frank." First they brought me to their Bible study group at one of their friends' homes, where we enjoyed a lovely dinner and time of fellowship. Perhaps we enjoyed it too much, as we realized so much time had slipped away, we would miss the opening of the play. Anna wasn't comfortable entering the theater late, especially since she'd purchased front-row seats. Understandably, she was disappointed and a bit perturbed.

I tried to console her as we drove home, but she had truly been looking forward to it. So had I. Quite a few years had passed since we shared the joy of watching a play together. When Anna, who was behind the wheel, pulled into the driveway, Kevin flew into the house. I thought maybe he needed to use the bathroom. Again I hugged Anna and tried to encourage her.

Inside the house Kevin greeted us, now wearing a scarf tied under his chin and clutching a journal (aka, a diary) to his chest. He proceeded to put his all into a one-man performance of the play we had missed. And, I might add, he was very good! At one point, he led Anna and me up the staircase into a room he called the "Anne Frank Room," while screaming, "The Nazis are coming! The Nazis are coming!"

By now Anna was leaning against the wall for support, holding her side, brimming with laughter. Then and there, I knew how deeply they loved each other and the lengths they would always go to for one another. They would be more than okay.

Would I come to adore our son-in-law, Kevin, over the years to follow? Let me count the ways. He was a churchgoing Jesus-lover, a man of prayer, a devoted husband, father, brother, and son. He tenderly cared for his Aunt Mary, who lived with dementia for several years, and he was great for conversation. Sometimes he was even willing to dance with me. Kevin was everything I hoped for and more!

I often missed Mom and Dad (Mom had passed in 2007 of congestive heart failure) and wished they could be around to meet their great grandchildren. In those times, I reminded myself I would be selfish to wish them back to earth. They had graduated from their worn-out earthly bodies to perfect bodies and perfect joy. What more could I wish for them?

Back when Dad retired and found he had more time on his hands, he took it on himself to compose a weekly devotion for his choir practice. I tucked all of his beautiful devotions away in my hope chest, thinking someday I would love to get them published, that the world may be blessed by Dad's heart of worship. This one was dated Thursday, February 16, 1994.

Music Hath Charms

Praise him with trumpet sound; praise him with lute and harp!

Psalm 150:3

Someone once wrote that "music hath charm to soothe the savage beast."

God spoke to Job of the morning stars singing together during the Creation, and in the book of Revelation we learn that in heaven ten thousand times ten thousand angels sing, while the whole creation joins in the chorus.

Music is all around us. While hiking on a deserted seashore, who cannot but be awed with the profound power and might of God, as he listens to the song of the waves fingering their way through the grains of sand. Who cannot sense God's love, as breezes undulate through the leaves of the trees in God's forests?

As new obstacles stand in the way of a babbling brook, its "song" intensifies. In similar manner, as our problems mount, the tempo of our songs of praise and exhortation to God increases. God hears and answers us. He understands our humanity, for he created us.

Praise the Lord with all instruments and songs, our bodies, and our every breath. And we have reason to praise him. Because of Jesus, our Lord and Savior. Let Psalm 150 help you to praise God!

Prayer for closing:

Dear Lord, tune up our hearts and voices and minds and instill in us the right spirit, that we can be counted on the roll of your heavenly choir.[7]

Music is all around us indeed. Today when I look up from my piano, my eyes land on a sign hanging there that once belonged to my dad. It reads, "For heights and depths no words can reach, music is the soul's own speech."

Music was there when I sat at the foot of Dad's favorite recliner, listening to him read his latest devotion. There, when I cut his hair. There, in his teasing. *Chrissy Emi, the day you blew into Long Beach sure was memorable.*

Music surrounded a devout Lutheran family, and a girl who wasn't at all Finnish and definitely wasn't sisu, but whose song intensified when problems mounted. Who discovered what Dad termed "the profound power and might of God" in her weakness.

I think of my childhood home and later my own homes, built on faith and laughter, trials and tears. And always, music.

When Dad had his stroke, my mom was given his personal effects for safekeeping. After he passed, she and I looked through his wallet. Tucked there among the items he always kept close, we found two tiny notes that touched me deeply. On one, he'd written his pet name for me, Chrissy Emi, along with my phone number at work.

The other contained a Bible verse.

Now faith is being sure of what we hope for and certain of what we do not see.

Hebrews 11:1 NIV 1984

Faith. Not fear. I believe Dad would have given his hearty approval of the title of his daughter's story.

Afterword

Marching Orders

⁓

B orn with sisu or not, I had acquired a fire in my belly. Maybe not for the kinds of things my parents would have chosen, but for those I believe God has. And I'm proud to be his soldier.

Until spring of 2017, Bob had always enjoyed good health, playing golf as weather permitted and a mean game of ping pong. But at eighty-four, he was diagnosed with a failing heart and bladder cancer requiring surgery to remove a large mass. After a horrible outpatient procedure to place a stent through his kidney and into his bladder, I feared Bob was falling through the cracks of the medical maize. His doctors were competent and well intentioned, but the right hand was definitely not talking to the left.

Time to put my hard-won assertiveness to work.

I contacted the triage nurse for his cardiologist, insisting Bob could not undergo the planned surgery unless his cardiologist saw him first. The cardiologist immediately called for an angiogram and discovered Bob's out-of-control atrial fibrillation. At last, cardiologist and urologist conferred and mutually agreed that Bob was in no shape for major surgery.

Later, after Bob had been on a new medication to stabilize his AFib, he was able to withstand the surgery, and he recovered well. Had we simply gone along with the plan, Bob may not have survived that procedure.

Recently, a door was opened for Mary, Bob, and I to move to Indianapolis, where Anna and Kevin both work as nurses while raising their two adorable children, Phoebe and Van. Together with their dog, Mardi, they lovingly welcomed us into their lives. Mary found a job doing social work, and I took a position in the VA hospital. Bob is still an emeritus with One America.

So now we're all together in one place! I give God the glory and thanks that this seemingly unattainable wish has become a reality.

Moving stirs memories. Four decades later, my breath still catches when I unwrap the tiny leg braces our dear Sarah wore. What a beautiful spirit she had, displaying love, laughter, and understanding beyond her chronical age. I often think about how her short life influenced each one of us. Even Anna, who never had the chance to meet her.

This thought transports me back to many years ago, when Anna was to perform a dramatic monologue for an acting and modeling competition held in downtown LA. My beautiful, statuesque, blonde-haired, blue-eyed daughter chose a script that cast her as a teenager curled up with contractures similar to someone with cerebral palsy. As fate would have it, Anna's performance was scheduled second to last, so she had to remain in character all day. For hours she sat huddled, dressed in a frumpy sweater from Sears and thick glasses. Only I and the students from her acting class knew she wasn't truly special needs.

When Anna's turn to perform finally came, I accompanied my "disabled" daughter to the stage. My heart skipped a beat when she fell down attempting to climb the stairs. This was not planned. But after sitting uncomfortably contracted for eight hours, she really did fall as she attempted the stairs. Anna stood tall, spoke clearly, and projected her voice before a panel of judges and a full room. I held my breath and prayed.

At a certain point in the monologue, Anna stopped speaking, dropped her hands to her sides, lowered her head, and stepped to the right, literally stepping out of character. There was a collective gasp in the room as she took off her glasses, shook her hair out of the ponytail, and spoke directly to the judges. I can't recall her exact words, but it was something like, "When you look at me, see who I am on the inside. I have feelings and emotions. I love to laugh and cry just like everyone else. See me for who I really am, who God made me to be." Then Anna stepped back into character, replaced her glasses, completed her monologue, and took a bow. The room exploded in applause and cheers. She won first place.

Mary has endured so much—the loss of Sarah, her parents' divorce, childhood cancer followed by a lifetime of pain-management issues, buying a home only to lose it in bankruptcy and foreclosure, job loss due to health problems, struggles with depression. Even a broken foot the night before we flew to Indianapolis for Anna and Kevin's wedding! But I thank God for his enduring mercies, for wonderful doctors who have helped keep Mary upright, and for her strong trust in Jesus Christ. She not only survived cancer, she has enjoyed a diverse career in social work, ministering to others who have to endure medical hardships.

Not long ago, I stopped in my tracks when I looked up at Mary's bookshelf. There sat the stuffed monkey Leslie gave Mary thirty-something years ago when she was hospitalized.

I still claim Leslie as my fourth daughter, and she's like a sister to both my girls. She and her mom, Nancy, remain our precious, close friends, and they're two of the funniest, most loving people I know.

Several summers ago, Mary, Anna, Kevin, and my grand-daughter Phoebe, then just sixteen months old, flew to Long Beach to spend the Fourth of July holiday with Leslie. We hit the beach and Disneyland, barbecued, and splashed in the blow-up pool in the backyard near the tent where Leslie and I slept at night. At the time, Anna was "great with child," wilting in the summer heat. Now Leslie is godmother to my grandson, Van Benjamin.

When Van was barely a toddler, Anna and Kevin attempted to reenact the traditional nativity scene with my two grand-children and two of their little friends. "Bampa Bob" read the Christmas story from Luke. Even Mardi the dog got in the act. Little Van carried the gifts for Jesus in his tiny hands. He kept walking away from the manger where one of Phoebe's dolls lay, saying "Wise man, wise man."

"Son, you need to give the gifts to the baby Jesus," said Kevin. So Van walked up and threw the gifts at "Jesus." Mean-while, Phoebe wore angel wings and proclaimed, "Do not be afraid!" Looking upset, her little friend named Archer, who played Joseph, turned to her. "I am *not* afraid! Do not say I am afraid. I am not afraid of anything!"

In the video on Facebook, Phoebe can be seen furiously stomping her foot and insisting, "That is not what you say!" We laughed until we cried. And I just kept thinking, *Oh, how Mom and Dad would have loved this.* Treasuring it up in my heart.

After Dad passed, my dear friend Juddie became my rock. Changing zip codes could never change the abiding friendship we share. Since birth, we have truly been through it all together—from the nursery at Bethany Lutheran and parochial school, to adolescence and young adulthood, to marriages and motherhood. I'm the proud godmother to her firstborn son, Brad. Juddie and I share our faith and our humor, and I can soldier on in part because God placed her in my life to always be there for me.

I recently read something that made me stop and think. The author reframed Eisenhower's D-Day speech in light of the spiritual battle we are fighting in these end times. Sounds right to me.

"There is a rising up," writes Mark Taylor, "a World War II component to the upcoming battle Christians will encounter as we take the ground for the Great Crusade in the Army of God. Heaven is upon you. We will bring about the destruction of the satanic war machine and the elimination of demonic tyranny over the free world!" For the body of Christ, he said, "now is the time to rewrite history. We will prevail. We will win!"[8]

I have now worked for the Veterans Health Administration for over a decade, and I've met veterans from almost every international war in which America has fought. My father served in the Merchant Marines on the Great Lakes during WWII and my first husband served four years in the Air Force, seeing duty in Vietnam. Bob served in the Army during the Korean War.

Taylor's article brought to mind a ninety-three-year-old gentleman I was privileged to meet back in 2011. Tall and lean and dressed impeccably, he used a walker as he entered my office at the prompting of his only child, a daughter living out of state. She was worried about his living alone and wanted the VA to provide him with an alert in case he fell or had an emergency. I invited the vet to tell me about his experience in WWII.

"You are too young to know anything about that war," he said. I encouraged him to share his stories if he was comfortable.

"On D-Day, I drove a tank onto the beach at Normandy. I was focused on our mission, but I must tell you there were many, many obstacles in our way—beams sticking up, and mines. I plowed through all that and made it all the way across France in my tank. Then there was another big battle called the Battle of the Bulge. You probably do not know about these events."

"Oh, sir, I have studied some WWII books that my parents kept in their library. I've also seen most war movies ever made. Please continue if you are able."

"Well," he went on, "we made it through Normandy and the Battle of the Bulge was underway and some Kraut jumped on my tank and threw a hand grenade, and I lit up like a Roman candle. I remember thinking, *I guess this is it now*. I prayed. The next thing I knew, one of my fellow buddies pulled me out of the tank. I spent a couple years in a burn unit in France.

"Finally, I made it back to the good old USA, married my sweetheart, had a great career and a good life. I buried my sweet wife of over sixty-three years a while back and now I have a girl-friend. Now my daughter wants me to move in with her, and I don't want to move to California!"

I laughed through tears and thanked him for his story. I ordered the alert, so his daughter would have some peace while he remained in Oregon, happily living out his life.

I think of this fine, dignified gentleman often as I work. We don't see many WWII vets these days, and they truly are the Greatest Generation. What a privilege I have to serve our veterans!

I believe Christians are experiencing spiritual warfare like never before. God is using ordinary people for his end-time harvest. His army is the winning side. We must be prayerful and alert. You and I are meant to have one heart, one mind, and be in one accord—to display unity, with all eyes on the mission, not the obstacles. Taking ground for the kingdom of God and holding it at all costs.

While I have never enrolled in the military, I am a lifer in the Army of God. I wrote this book because Jesus, my general, gave me my orders. *Tell the world, Chrissy Emi. I am real. I hear their prayers. Never fear, I watch over my sheep. I am here!*

Satan isn't long for this world, and he knows it.

Through all the trials I have endured on my journey and all the blessings I have enjoyed, I have won the peace that passes understanding. The love of Jesus, my Savior. And everlasting life! I shouldn't be here to tell my story. Even having escaped the abortionist, I can only give one explanation for my ongoing survival through those cold and shadowy valleys. My God always made a way . . . because that's what he does. He can be counted on to make our steps sure, our hearts tender, and our souls sing.

For you as for me, he'll never waste a sliver of pain. He will always redeem the worst and, ultimately, reveal the best. His plan is victory, and it can be trusted.

I pray my story nourishes your faith and reassures you that despite our chaotic world, God is alive and in control. GPYW. With God's plan, you win!

May the God of hope fill you with all joy and peace as you trust in him, so that you may overflow with hope by the power of the Holy Spirit.

Romans 15:13 NIV

Be strong and courageous with your faith. Be a light to those in darkness!

God bless you all.

END NOTES

1. "Our Finnish Heritage," Finlandia University, November 2019, https://www.finlandia.edu/about/our-finnish-heritage/.

2. "Miss Anna Sofia Turja," Encyclopedia Titanica, November 2019, https://www.encyclopedia-titanica.org/titanic-survivor/anna-sofia-turja.html.

3. "Titanic Survivor Story – Anna Turja Lundi's Experience," Titanic Universe, November 2019, http://www.titanicuniverse.com/titanic-survivor-story-turja/1039.

4. Joseph Medlicott Scriven, "What a Friend We Have in Jesus," public domain.

5. Charles Dickens, *A Christmas Carol*, (New York: Atria Books, 2013).

6. C. S. Lewis, *The Problem of Pain*, revised ed. (New York: Harper One, 2015).

7. Mickey Lundi, "Music Hath Charms," dated Feb. 16, 1994, from his collected devotions, previously unpublished.

8. Mark Taylor, "Army of God," Mark Taylor Prophecies, June 6, 2015, http://www.angelfire.com/ks/landzastanza/messages.html#03.

A sweet sister moment—Anna, so gorgeous and excited with her sister Mary in front of the altar and purple backdrop Anna had made by hand. Mary had fallen and broken her foot the night before we flew to Indiana for the wedding. Mary was in a wheelchair. Mary was Anna's maid of honor. Thank God that Mary could muster up the courage and determination to stand up next to Anna for this picture. Anna's excitement and happiness are palpable in this picture. It was precious to me to see Anna and Mary looking at each other on this beautiful day!

This moment is forever etched onto my heart. My Anna Marie, my youngest daughter, my gift from God, getting ready to have her dad, Tom, walk her down the aisle to marry Kevin. We were in the bride's room at the church. There were other people in the room, but for these brief minutes it was only Anna and I having a sweet mother-daughter bridal moment. It was an intimate moment, where I gave thanks for her being born, thanks for God affirming her birth, thanks for she and Kevin being brought together by the Lord, and a reminder for her to cherish this day. I said, "You are so beautiful, and I am so happy for you! I love you Anna!"

Beautiful Brianna is holding one of the twins she had just delivered. I love
the divine joy radiating from her blue eyes and her smile. Brianna is exuding
her fulfillment and happiness in serving Christ in Africa, where He called
her to serve. Working as a midwife in a mission hospital was challenging, but
Brianna served God with her whole heart!

Graduating with my master's degree in social work was just the beginning of my journey to serve God's people! I felt relief and excitement on this day in August. I give thanks for Bob; he and my parents were fully supportive of this undertaking. As I reflect on my years in social work, I still marvel how the Lord used me to actually become the social worker at Long Beach Memorial Hospital working at the Geraldine Stramski Center with the families of spina bifida children and many other types of birth anomalies. I also give thanks that on this journey I met four people who I love and revere: Judy, Sandy, Thomas, and Donna.

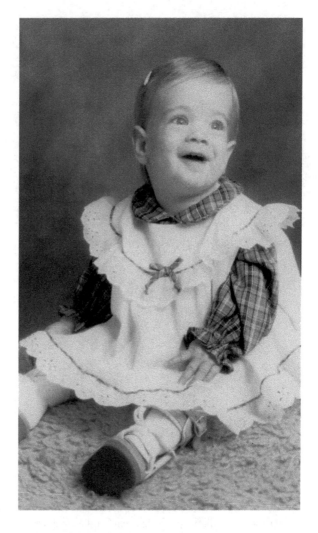

Sarah, my little angel. So full of joy and wonder. I imagine her beautiful green eyes to be looking at Jesus in her heavenly home. I have her little leg braces and shoes stored lovingly away in my hope chest. Sarah brought laughter, comfort, and inspiration to everyone she encountered in her short twenty-three-and-a-half-month life on Earth. God made her just for me to fulfill His special purpose in life's cycle of timeless dreams. I know that some-day I will be reunited with my sweet daughter.